AF223885

attention is given to the task of multiplying, these two widely respected veterans have crafted a field guide to looking after the person of the multiplier themselves.
–Peyton Jones
CEO New Breed Training
Author of *Discipology: The Art and Science of Making Disciples*

Larry is a leader who carries both the clarity of a visionary and the deeply pastoral heart of a shepherd. He leads with intentionality and consistently points people toward faithfulness over visibility. **That same conviction shapes this book, calling leaders to multiply disciples and leave a Kingdom legacy that actually lasts.**
–Dhati Lewis
President, MyBLVD
Visionary Pastor, Blueprint Church

The Making of a Multiplier reframes Christian leadership around what matters most: developing and empowering Christlike leaders with a multiplication mindset. **Walkemeyer and Teter's four season framework—spring, summer, autumn, winter—offers profound insight into how God shapes leaders across a lifetime.** Using Barnabas as their model, they show that legacy isn't built through visibility but through faithful investment in others. The book's central challenge is both convicting and hopeful: multiplication is a way of life cultivated through every season. **Essential reading for any leader asking, "What is my legacy?"**
–Dr. Bruce Wilson
Director, The Center for Church Multiplication at Asbury Theological Seminary

In *The Making of a Multiplier*, Larry Walkemeyer and John Teter provide a counter-cultural roadmap for leaders who want their impact to outlive their tenure. By utilizing a four-season framework, the authors move beyond growth metrics to explore how God shapes a leader's soul over a lifetime. Rooted in the life of Barnabas, the research of Dr. Robert Clinton, and decades of their own ministry experience, **Walkemeyer and Teter offer a masterclass in finishing well. This book is a must-read for any leader ready to trade the math of addition for the lasting Kingdom legacy of multiplication.**
–Dr. Adam J. Morris
President, Azusa Pacific University

Walkemeyer and Teter—two seasoned ministry veterans—challenge us to think about the discipleship multiplication impact of our own ministries. **Particularly insightful is the use of the four seasons to help the reader diagnose their own stage in ministry to maximize Kingdom potential. A must-read for any Christian leader who wants to "winter" well!**
–Dr. Jon Braunersreuther
President, Texas District of The Lutheran Church—Missouri Synod

What a breath of fresh air! Like their man Barnabas, whom they bring to life comprehensively, Larry and John pour out encouragement. **With personal authenticity and biblical insights, they explore the four seasons of life. From their vantage points of autumn and winter, they celebrate the hard-won wisdom of these**

maturing-but-still-fruitful seasons. This book frees me to unapologetically own that I'm now in winter, and consider the gifts I can pass on to others while I "run to the finish line." A quick but powerful read!
–Dr. Linda Adams
Bishop, Free Methodist Church of Canada

The Making of a Multiplier is a much-needed book that helps leaders understand the rhythms of life and leadership that lead to multiplication rather than just addition. I've long admired Robert Clinton's insightful work, and Larry Walkemeyer and John Teter in this book extend it further for a new generation. **I genuinely believe it's an essential read for all leaders who desire to multiply leadership.**
–Tim O'Neil
Director, Exponential Australia

The Making of a Multiplier is a timely guide for pastors and leaders who yearn to create impact that outlives them. With biblical depth and practical wisdom, **Larry and John masterfully use the four seasons of spring, summer, autumn and winter to show how God forges leaders over the course of a lifetime, drawing powerfully from the life of Barnabas.** This book challenges leaders to finish well, multiply disciples, and steward every season to leave a lasting Kingdom legacy.
–Will Plitt
Executive Director, Christ Together

As a denominational leader shaped by the Wesleyan conviction that God's grace forms us over a lifetime, I am constantly asking how we cultivate leaders who don't merely grow ministries but faithfully multiply the mission. *The Making of a Multiplier* gave language and biblical clarity to that burden, reminding me that true fruitfulness flows from formation, humility, and faithful stewardship across every season of leadership. **Larry Walkemeyer and John Teter have written a timely and deeply helpful guide for leaders who desire to finish well and leave a lasting, Spirit-empowered Kingdom legacy.**
–Dr. Ed Love
Executive Director of Church Multiplication and Discipleship, The Wesleyan Church

This is an important book for this moment. As the Church faces multiple challenges and the limitations of traditional approaches to ministry, *The Making of a Multiplier* offers a hopeful and deeply biblical reorientation. Larry Walkemeyer and John Teter lay out a compelling vision for reclaiming our apostolic heritage by re-defining leadership around multiplication rather than addition. I especially resonated with the "seasons of leadership" and its application through the life of Barnabas—one of Scripture's quiet but most catalytic multipliers. **This book calls us away from building platforms and toward forming people. Its message is hopeful, challenging, and exactly what the Church needs right now.**
–Raj Pillai
Vice President/Chief of Staff, Exponential

The message of this book is an important one for the days that we are living in. While we see increased spiritual curiosity in younger generations, we have fewer leaders being prepared to disciple them into the future. **I have met many of the leaders that Larry Walkemeyer has invested in and witnessed their fruitfulness, so I know he is uniquely qualified to write this book with John Teeter, who is doing the same.** My prayer is that more of us want to be like Barnabas.

–Kaye Kolde
Bishop, Free Methodist Church USA

As I continue to lead through different seasons of church ministry and organizational leadership, I carry a growing hunger to hear from those ahead of me who have proven their perspective through effective practice and godly perseverance. This book's work, forming a view through four seasons of life and leadership, delivers a nuanced perspective that is helping me now as I step into next seasons. And, having these truths delivered from people who have walked this out personally, while maintaining a deep love for and connection to the local church, and who hold my respect, adds to my interest to listen and learn. **My life and leadership has already benefited from the principles in this book, and I believe yours will as well.**

–Jason Shepperd
Founder, Church Project

It's been a privilege to see Larry Walkemeyer embody what it means to be a healthy disciple-making leader who champions reproduction in leadership environments both locally, nationally,

and beyond. ***The Making of a Multiplier* is more than a book—it's a roadmap for you and your team to thrive relationally, physically, mentally, and spiritually while making a lasting Kingdom impact.** As we pursue The 16% Mission, this resource provides the practical principles and inspiration needed to multiply leaders and leave a legacy that outlives you. **Don't just read this book—dive into it with your team and start multiplying today!**
–Jason Stewart
Executive Director for Mobilization, Exponential

***The Making of a Multiplier* is the guide that I wish I had 30 years ago.** Yet, no matter our stage in life, it offers meaning and hope for today. Walkemeyer and Teter help us see our lives through the lens of legacy, while providing a perspective that enables us to live meaningfully in the moment.
–Rev. Dr. Steve Cordle
Director of Church Multiplication, Global Methodist Church
Executive Director, The River Network International

The Making of a Multiplier is a wise, biblical, and practical book for leaders at every stage. Drawing on themes from Dr. J. Robert Clinton's classic ***The Making of a Leader* for a new generation, Larry and John share personal stories, deep Scriptural insight, and crisp challenges that foster growth and maturation. A fun, engaging, and powerful read.**
–Alex and Hannah Absalom
Directors, Dandelion Resourcing

In a world that often measures success by personal achievement, *The Making of a Multiplier* presents a powerful counter-narrative, focusing on exponential impact and enduring legacy. The four-seasons framework provides a strategic blueprint for intentional development and investment, both personally and in others. **This book challenges us to think beyond short-term gains, encouraging a deep, long-term strategic investment in people that yields an immeasurable return for God's Kingdom.**
–Bill Couchenour
Director of Deployment, Exponential

The Making of a Multiplier is a refreshing look at how God shapes leaders over a lifetime. The four-seasons framework reminds me that lasting leadership isn't just about what I accomplish, but who I empower. **With clear and biblical insights, this book is an essential guide for leaders who want to discern their current season, multiply their impact, and finish well.**
–Dr. JR Rushik
Director, Church Development Network
Superintendent, Acts 12:24 Conference

The Making of a Multiplier is not a leadership book chasing the next idea. It is a wise, pastoral guide shaped by decades of faithful ministry and a deep trust in how God forms leaders over time. Larry Walkemeyer and John Teter write with the clarity of people who have finished many races and are now helping others finish well. This book reframes success around health, season, and legacy—and calls leaders back to the quiet, powerful work of multiplication. **In a moment hungry for**

shortcuts, this is a timely invitation to depth, faithfulness, and fruit that lasts.
–Rob Wegner
Co-Founder and Director, the KC Underground
Mobilization and Practice Catalyst, Exponential
Co-author of *Starfish and the Spirit.*

As I approach the end of my autumn season and aim to leave a lasting legacy, I truly appreciate Larry Walkemeyer and John Teter's book, *The Making of a Multiplier.* It resonates with my strong desire to make a meaningful impact—to live a life that leaves a lasting mark beyond my time. **Psalm 90:12 reminds us, "So teach us to number our days, that we may gain a heart of wisdom." This book is a guiding light to that wisdom."**
–Jeff Matas
Executive State Pastor, Indiana Church of God

Most leadership books celebrate summer—the season of growth and visibility. This one honors winter. Walkemeyer and Teter offer a profoundly counter-cultural vision: legacy is built not by what you accumulate but by what you release. **The sobering research on finishing well alone makes this essential reading. If you want your influence to outlast your title, start here.**
–Rob Douglas,
District Superintendent, Central Pacific District,
The Christian and Missionary Alliance

In *The Making of a Multiplier*, Larry Walkemeyer and John Teter
remind us that leadership isn't lived in a straight line; it moves
in seasons. Through the imagery of spring, summer, autumn
and winter, they show how God uses every season, from pruning
to harvest, to shape a leader's spiritual health and ability
to multiply others. **As you read, you'll likely spot your
current season, smile (or wince) at past ones, and sense
God already at work in what's ahead. I found it both
insightful and encouraging.** Every season, it turns out, is
part of God's faithful work of forming fruitful leaders.
–Noemi Chavez
Lead Pastor, Revive Church
Speaker

Many conversations around multiplication focus on starting
well: a new believer's conversion, a new leader commissioned,
a new church's launch. Strong starts are worth celebrating, for
sure! But like a first spark without a stack of firewood nearby,
we've all seen far too many examples of the flames dying
prematurely. This book addresses that tension, asking what it
looks like to finish well! Larry Walkemeyer and John Teter are in
different seasons of life and ministry, and their unique perspec-
tives invite faithful men and women in every season to consider
various aspects of holistic health, in the various seasons of life
everyone walks through. **Their insights, examples, and
lessons will serve you well, no matter where you are in
your leadership journey. And** *The Making of a Multiplier*
**just might be the tool that God would use to help you
finish well.**
–Ben Connelly
Founder, The Equipping Group
Servant Leadership Team, Salt+Light Community

There are a number of excellent ministry books on your current reading list. This book should immediately move to the front of that line. Why? Because Larry and John are going to help you with your biggest challenge—leading your ministry into disciple-maker multiplication as the central rhythm of your life and ministry. And the "season" God has you in right now is part of what he wants to use to see disciples multiplied through you. The adventure, and ministry, you're dreaming of is on the other side of what *The Making of a Multiplier* is going to unpack for you.
–**Eric Creekmore**
Lead Pastor, Lakeview Bible Church

How many leaders can honestly say their local church has planted more churches than it has parking spots? That credential alone should compel all ministry leaders to take Larry's words seriously. Larry is not just a theorist but a fruitful practitioner in every way. Across local church leadership, denominational influence, church-planting networks, and Christian higher education, Larry has demonstrated that authentic Kingdom growth always prioritizes depth over breadth. Larry's words were formed in the trenches of real-life ministry, and he practices what he preaches like very few I have ever encountered.
–**Brad Goode**
Lead Pastor, Good News Church, Santa Rosa Beach

The Making of a Multiplier **is a timely, wise, and deeply formational work that reorients Christian leadership away from scale and toward lasting fruit.** With biblical depth and lived credibility, Walkemeyer and Teter remind us that multiplication is not a strategy but a way of life stewarded across seasons. This book challenges leaders to discern their season, release control, and invest faithfully in others so the Kingdom continues to grow long after they are gone.

–Dave Slater
Ministries Director, Western Ontario District,
Pentecostal Assemblies of Canada

THE MAKING OF A MULTIPLIER

FOUR SEASONS TO MAXIMIZE YOUR KINGDOM LEGACY

LARRY WALKEMEYER &
JOHN TETER

EXPONENTIAL

Exponential is a growing movement of activists committed to the multiplication of healthy new churches. Exponential Resources spotlights actionable principles, ideas, and solutions for the accelerated multiplication of healthy, reproducing faith communities. For more information, visit exponential.org.

The Making of a Multiplier: Four Seasons to Maximize Your Kingdom Legacy

ISBN: 978-1-62424-138-3 (paperback)
ISBN: 978-1-62424-139-0 (ebook/epub)
Editor: Karen Cain
Cover and interior design: Lisa DeSelm

With Profound Gratitude

To Deb Walkemeyer,
who has gracefully loved me through the four seasons of my life and shown
me what the spirit of Barnabas looks like in a leader.

To Becky Teter,
Thank you for being grace upon grace (John 1:16) to me.
It is a joy and honor to follow Jesus with you.
God is faithful in each and every season.

The Making of A Multiplier: Four Seasons to Maximize Your Kingdom Legacy

FOREWORD

After more than four decades in full-time ministry, I've come to believe that one of the most important questions a leader can ask is not "What difference am I making?" but "What am I passing on so others can take it from here and multiply?"

In fact, Jesus framed leadership this way. On the night before his death, he told his disciples that they would do even greater things after he was gone. That was not a statement about ambition or scale, but about trust. He entrusted his work, his teaching, and his mission to others, believing they would carry it forward beyond his own time and ministry.

That is the heart of multiplication, and it is the vision this book so faithfully recovers.

Through the years, I've learned that what endures is rarely the work we do ourselves. Far more valuable are the transferable truths and wisdom we share with others, forged through experience, failure, faithfulness, and grace. These help others avoid unnecessary missteps and build upon what has already been learned. When stewardship replaces ownership, leadership shifts from personal legacy to Kingdom multiplication.

Yet beneath this aspirational vision lies something deeply human. Each of us carries two fundamental needs: we want to know that our lives matter, and we want to know that we are loved. Stated another way, we have a deep-seated need for significance and security—to contribute something meaningful and to belong, to make a difference, and to be appreciated along the way.

Healthy multiplication honors both. It allows our lives to count beyond ourselves while rooting leadership in adaptive practices shaped by wisdom rather than in temporary platforms chasing visibility and influence.

Just after I turned 50, a mentor said to me, "Mark, you're rounding second base." He went on to explain that life is much like a baseball diamond.

From birth to roughly age 25, we ***learn***. As we run toward first base, we begin discovering who we are, who we're not, and the purposes for which God intends to use us.

From roughly age 25 to 50, as we run from first to second base. We ***do***. We take risks, build, and lead, often measuring success by position, productivity, and visible results.

From roughly age 50 to 75, as we run from second to third base, we ***teach***. Here the calling begins to shift. Faithful stewardship requires us to move away from being the primary actor to empowering others.

And from age 75 onward, as we round third base and head toward home, the aim is to ***finish well***, leaving a legacy that benefits others and brings glory to God.

Of course, life and leadership are never this linear. Every season includes moments of failure, disappointment, struggle, and loss. I have known each personally. What separates those who finish well from those who do not is not the absence of hardship, but a refusal to quit on God, on your family, on yourself, on your calling, or on the people God has entrusted to you. And when you come out the other side of challenging chapters, you carry something precious to pass on as well: wisdom seasoned by suffering and hope forged through perseverance. That, too, is meant to be multiplied.

The parable of the talents (Matthew 25:14-30) may focus on money, but the principle reaches far beyond finances. Everything entrusted to us—including spiritual gifts, natural talents, cultivated aptitude, time, and relationships—should be leveraged to multiply God's Kingdom and equip others to do the same.

This is where *The Making of a Multiplier* speaks with refreshing clarity. In a ministry culture often driven by performance, metrics, and celebrity, Larry and John point us to a biblical and actionable vision of stewardship. They write not as theorists, but as proven practitioners passing on wisdom shaped by lived experience.

To be clear, multiplication is not something you pursue someday. It is something faithful leaders practice in every season of their life and ministry—in spring, summer, autumn, and winter, as the authors encourage. You *learn* with transfer in mind. You *do* with stewardship in mind. You *teach* with intentional release in mind. And you *finish well* by trusting God to do through others what you could never accomplish alone.

So, what are you stewarding in this season of your life and ministry? What are you passing on so others can build upon it and multiply? When these questions guide us, significance is discovered, security is established, and the Kingdom of God advances beyond the scope of any one leader, church, or generation.

That is the mission of multiplication. And that is a vision and a leadership trajectory worthy of our full commitment.

–Dr. Mark DeYmaz
Founding Pastor and Directional Leader, **Mosaic Church of Central Arkansas**
Author, **Building a Healthy Multiethnic Church** and **Make Me an Instrument of Your Peace**

INTRODUCTION
Defining a True Multiplier

There is a time for everything, and a season for every activity under the heavens: a time to be born and a time to die.
–Ecclesiastes 3:1-2

The Church has a math problem it must solve. Making multipliers is the solution—the biblical solution.

Imagine this: One ordinary follower of Jesus chooses to be made into a multiplier. They commit to three years of discipling just three individuals. It feels slow, almost insignificant. But multiplication is hidden in small beginnings. After those first three years, the original disciple-maker plus their three disciples now total four. If each of them then takes on three new disciples for the next three years, the number grows to 12 disciple-makers after six years—still unimpressive at first glance.

Yet something powerful has begun. Continue this simple pattern—each person discipling three for three years—and by year 12, the movement reaches 256 disciples. That number is larger than 92% of all churches in America.[1] Repeat the pattern, and the numbers quickly become staggering. By year 18, the movement reaches 4,096 disciples—twice the size of a megachurch. And it happens with no worship band, no lights, no building, no pulpit, no events, no budget, and no insurance. Just simple, Jesus-style disciple-making that maximizes their Kingdom legacy. Such exponential potential is why Jesus chose multiplication for his ministry model. We must follow his model to reach the world.

---

[1] Thom S. Rainer, "Five Major Developments for Churches with an Attendance Under 250," *Church Answers*, January 2024, accessed November 23, 2025.

Your Unique "Season Story"

What is your unique "season story"? What season of life are you in? Are you developing your "maximum Kingdom impact" life during each of your seasons? John and I believe this book can significantly increase your impact—and help you inspire others to increase theirs. You can be a multiplier!

I am in my winter season. John is in autumn. We are both seeking to learn the vital lessons God has for us in the season we are in. We are both committed to being multipliers leading maximum-impact lives. Over time, multipliers produce the most Kingdom harvest. They leave an expanding and enduring legacy.

The four seasons of a year help us picture the major phases of a lifetime. In the natural realm, each season brings unique beauty, blessings, and challenges. Similarly, each season of life carries specific opportunities, lessons, milestones, and missions. Understanding *your* seasons can propel you to higher levels of personal health and ministry fruitfulness.

Our aim in these pages is to give you a 30,000-foot-level view of your life seasons. We will share key insights that the Holy Spirit seeks to teach us during each season. You will reflect on the seasons you have come through, better understand the season you are currently in, and prepare to be faithful and fruitful for the remaining seasons of life.

Whatever your age or season, knowing where you are and what's ahead is wisdom. Season awareness is wisdom: "Go to the ant, you sluggard; consider its ways and be wise! It has no commander, no overseer or ruler, yet it stores its provisions in summer and gathers its food at harvest" (Proverbs 6:6–8).

John and I want to help you write your "season story" so it ends with a testimony of deep faithfulness and maximum fruit. The hard news is that you can't change any past seasons in your story. The hopeful news is that you can start today, in your current season, and write a greater story—the story of a multiplier.

Your Four Seasons

Jesus, speaking first of himself, then of those who follow him, declares, "Very truly I tell you, unless a kernel of wheat falls to the ground and dies, it remains only a single seed. But if it dies, it produces many seeds" (John 12:24). The wheat seed only multiplies if it goes through the four seasons God designed for it. It must 1) be planted, 2) grow, 3) be harvested, and 4) then multiply as some of its seed is replanted. In a similar way, God is seeking to shape us into multipliers through all the seasons of our lives.

You have a unique season story. Your SPRING is when God PLANTS your identity. Your SUMMER is God GROWING your ministry effectiveness. AUTUMN is your life maturing into HARVEST productivity. WINTER brings the final season of legacy, or REPLANTING into the lives of those who will multiply God's Kingdom after you go home.

Your seasons are not defined by your chronological age (although, there are general ages at which these seasons usually occur). Instead, these seasons are marked by what Dr. Robert Clinton calls major development stages. Each stage is full of certain elements: God-provided people, events, experiences, and even tests that shape a leader over time. Often "boundary events" mark the transition from one season to the next.[2]

---

[2] Clinton, Robert J. *The Making of a Leader: Recognizing the Lessons and Stages of Leadership Development.* Colorado Springs: NavPress, 1988.

For most leaders, an approximate age for each development seasons is: spring, 0–30; summer, 25–50; autumn, 45–65; winter, 60+. (Overlap is intentional.)

John began his spring season (age 0–25) in Los Angeles. He grew up in a bi-racial Wasian home. He became a disciple of Jesus at age 22 while a college student at UCLA. Summer (age 25–45) was broken up into two halves: as a campus minister at USC, Cal State Dominguez Hills and Compton College, and as a church planter and denominational leader for church planting and evangelism. He is currently in autumn (age 49–64) and age 55 at the time of this writing.

My spring season (age 0–25) was spent in "Smallville," Kansas (living near Clark Kent), then urban Los Angeles. My summer season (age 25-49) was as a youth pastor in Seattle and young lead pastor in Long Beach. My autumn (age 49–64) was as a mature pastor in Long Beach and staff member of Exponential. Winter (age 64+) is underway as I promote multiplication in a national role with our denomination and serving with Exponential. I don't anticipate any major development or organizational shifts. I just pray that God will add more Holy Spirit fuel to develop leaders and help them finish well.

This is the deployment reality of our different seasons. The most important part of any season story is what God is developing in us through each one, as he teaches us and shapes us to become Kingdom multipliers.

Robert J. Clinton's *The Making of a Leader* provides a widely used framework for understanding how God shapes leaders over time through experience, calling, and response. Clinton's emphasis on leadership development as a lifelong, God-directed process—including identifiable stages and formative lessons—serves as a primary reference point throughout this book. The present work engages Clinton's model as a guiding framework while integrating biblical theology, contemporary leadership scholarship, and practical ministry experience across varied contexts.

The Seasons of Barnabas

One of the most fruitful Kingdom leaders in the New
Testament is largely unknown and often forgotten. Remember
Barnabas? How many books have you read about him? Neither
John nor I could recall more than one sermon on Barnabas in
a lifetime of churchgoing. Yet, there may not have been a Paul
without a Barnabas. We might not have had the Antioch church
or the Book of Mark. Barnabas never wanted to be a hero, but
he was passionate about being a hero maker. This is the heart of
a multiplier.

Jim Collins, the renowned leadership author of *Good to Great*,
writes "Level 5 leaders never wanted to become larger-than-life
heroes. They never aspired to be put on a pedestal or become
unreachable icons."[3]

Most of us have a hard time seeing ourselves as the apostle
Paul, but almost all of us can picture being a Barnabas. Collins
continues writing about maximum impact leaders: "Our culture
is drawn to the idea of the 'great leader'—the larger-than-life
charismatic hero. Yet the leaders of good-to-great companies
were remarkable for their lack of celebrity"[4] (*Good to Great*, p. 30).

Our church culture has created a hyper-focus on celebrity
leaders. Sadly, this emphasis often has a demoralizing impact
on the 70% of pastors who will never lead a church of over 100

---

[3] Jim Collins, *Good to Great: Why Some Companies Make the Leap… and Others Don't*
(New York: HarperBusiness, 2001), 39–40. Collins describes Level 5 leaders
as marked by a paradoxical blend of personal humility and professional will,
intentionally avoiding celebrity status, hero narratives, or personal glorification
in favor of building enduring institutions.

[4] Jim Collins, *Good to Great: Why Some Companies Make the Leap… and Others Don't*
(New York: HarperBusiness, 2001), 12–13.

people.[5] Too often pastors are chasing the siren song of addition while missing the quiet power of multiplication.

As the ultimate multiplier, Barnabas models a different path to Kingdom impact and legacy. By studying and applying the season story of Barnabas, we can better understand how God shapes multipliers through the seasons of life and discover the path available to each of us.

Defining a Multiplier

How would you define a multiplier? Stop. We mean it. We want to know. More importantly we want YOU to know.

When you say "multiplier" what do you mean, and do you want to be one? Is the answer clear to you? Does it stir energy in your spirit, imagination in your mind, satisfaction in your soul? Is it doable (with the Spirit's assistance, of course)? Is it a big enough dream for your life?

When we titled our book *The Making of a Multiplier*, we wanted to be crystal clear about who God is making you into and what he is shaping you to do. While there's no one "right" definition, we believe Exponential's definition of a multiplier captures the essence of God's intent:

A multiplier is a healthy disciple-making leader who champions reproduction.

Let's introduce the three key concepts within this brief definition.

---

[5] https://www.churchleadership.com/leading-ideas/6-ways-forward-for-very-small-congregations/?utm_source=chatgpt.com (accessed 11-22-2025)

1) Healthy

How many of us know an unhealthy Christian leader? Actually, sadly, that is the wrong question. How many Christian leaders do we know who are unhealthy? Don't start counting unless you want a discouragement attack.

The emphasis on *healthy* underlines the essential reality that a multiplier is first characterized and known by personal identity, not public ministry. It is an acknowledgment that "we teach what we know, but we reproduce who we are." [6]

This health is multi-dimensional. The acrostic RPMS can help us grasp the basics of health. Just as a car has more power at higher RPMS, so do Christian leaders. These RPMS questions can be used for a daily health checkup:

R – Relational health: Am I investing in healthy, life-giving relationships?

P – Physical health: Am I caring for my body with rest, nutrition, movement, and margin?

M – Mental health: Am I feeding my mind with beauty, goodness, and truth? Am I processing my emotions with honesty, clarity, and assistance?

S – Spiritual health: Am I deepening my knowledge and experience in the truth, presence, and power of God? Am I prioritizing growing in the fruit of the Spirit and ministering from the power of the Spirit?

---

[6] Quote widely attributed to John C. Maxwell, used in various leadership teachings and consistent with themes in *Developing the Leader Within You 2.0* (HarperCollins Leadership, 2018).

Multipliers are never perfect. Barnabas wasn't. But they are healthy and fit to be imitated. They don't wait until they are fully mature to multiply, but they are ardently pursuing maturity and health while doing so.

Multipliers invite a few disciples close enough to catch the fire. This is a vulnerable place because in your personal space, they can see your warts and blemishes. It's also vulnerable because at this distance, they can stab you in the back or wound you deeply. But it's also the place of transparency and transmission. Your true fire is felt, and the flame is passed on.

Health to the Finish Line

My track coach was adamant about one key to racing: "Run through the tape!" In other words, "Don't quit before the race is over. Hit the tape at full speed!" It's what the apostle Paul declared: "I have finished the race, I have kept the faith" (2 Timothy 4:7).

An essential trait of a healthy multiplier is the determination to finish well. Legendary professor, Dr. Robert Clinton did the most prolific and respected research on Christian leaders who finished well. His shocking findings revealed that only one out of three do so.[7]

Clinton's definition of finishing well includes six vital characteristics: 1) a vibrant relationship with God; 2) a lifetime of learning; 3) Christlike character; 4) truth lived out; 5) lasting contributions (legacy); and 6) a sense of destiny being fulfilled.[8]

---

[7] J. Robert Clinton, *The Making of a Leader: Recognizing the Lessons and Stages of Leadership Development* (Colorado Springs, CO: NavPress, 1988), 17–20.

[8] J. Robert Clinton, *The Making of a Leader: Recognizing the Lessons and Stages of Leadership Development* (Colorado Springs, CO: NavPress, 1988), 108–137.

We will focus much more on these "finishing well" concepts throughout the book.

2) Disciple-making leader

Multipliers give priority to Jesus' call for all believers to pursue disciple-making (Matthew 28:19-20). Multipliers understand that this is Jesus' method of reaching the world. Jesus-style, life-on-life discipleship is not an optional accessory. We treat disciple-making like it's the sound system in our car. Actually, it is the tires. The most powerful car won't go anywhere until we put the tires on it. Discipleship is where the rubber meets the road, where we get traction for the mission.

Churches pursue their worship, sermons, small groups, programs, events, etc. All these can be good things, but they aren't the main thing. Jesus said, "Make disciples." If we do what he told *us* to do, we can trust him to do what he promised *he* would do: build the Church.

Multipliers understand that their maximum Kingdom impact in leadership won't be running programs or preaching sermons that go viral or gaining followers on social media. The leadership that leaves the largest legacy will be influencing individuals to become disciples who make disciples.

The word *leader* in the definition is important to understand. The study of leadership became very popular in Christian culture as church growth became the end goal. There is much to be commended in the wisdom and resources produced around leadership. The downside comes as the emphasis on leadership unintentionally demotes and obscures discipleship.

Are all Christians called to be leaders? We would say "yes" and "no." It all depends on how you define a leader. If you define it as John Maxwell does, "Leadership is influence—nothing more, nothing less," then "yes."[9] Why? Because all believers are called to make disciples, and that is intentional influence.[10] Are all believers called to be group or ministry or organizational leaders? No.

3) Champions reproduction

Multipliers are zealous for seeing reproduction actually happen. When you champion something, you are doing more than just agreeing with it; you are taking on a leadership role in its defense and promotion. You are investing your credibility, time, resources, and energy to ensure the advancement of what you believe in.

Multipliers aren't satisfied with attracting attendees; they want disciples who reproduce disciples. Their highest joy is not raising up leaders to run their programs; they desire to see leaders who propagate leaders. They aren't asking, "How big is our church?" but "How many churches have we birthed?"

They seek to become champions *in* multiplication and champions *for* multiplication. They multiply personal disciples. They personally apprentice and mentor leaders. They sacrificially send leaders and teams out to start new churches. They also encourage, support, highlight, and resource other leaders outside their direct influence and tribe. They'd rather hold the spotlight than stand in it. For multipliers, it is all about maximizing Kingdom impact—not about likes, followers, friends, subscribers, or contacts.

On earth, Jesus was the ultimate multiplier, the prime illustration of this definition. He was healthy. He is described as

---

[9] John C. Maxwell, *Developing the Leader Within You* (Nashville: Thomas Nelson, 1993), 1.

[10] Kerry Patterson, Joseph Grenny, David Maxfield, Ron McMillan, and Al Switzler, *Crucial Influence: Leadership Skills to Create Lasting Behavior Change*, 2nd ed. (New York: McGraw-Hill, 2013), 13.

growing in "wisdom and in stature, and in favor with God and with all people" (Luke 2:52). He had high RPMS. Jesus spent 75% of his ministry time in personal disciple-making. He led in other ministry expressions, but he focused on discipling. He championed reproduction, making it his first call (Matthew 4:19) and his last commission (28:16-20). Multiplicative disciple-making was his plan A to reach the world. He had no plan B.

Jesus had just three years of public ministry to start a global movement. What did he do? He chose the crockpot instead of the microwave. He trained his disciples to become multipliers! He focused on a few to reach the masses. He knew that a small group of multiplying disciples was bigger than the largest crowd of spectators.

The Beauty of All Skate

I felt marginalized at the roller rink when I was growing up in my small Kansas town. I couldn't skate backward when the rink DJ announced it was time for "backwards skate." I didn't have a girlfriend for the "couples skate." I couldn't skate fast enough when it was time for "fast skate." I wasn't over 18 yet, so I didn't qualify for the "adult skate." I just had to sit there. But you know I was waiting for the announcer to call out "ALL skate!" That was when I could finally get off the bench and get on the rink.

When Jesus gave his momentous mission invitation to "go make disciples," it was an "all skate" call! Everyone was expected to get on the rink and go for it. Soon after Jesus' invite, he poured out his Spirit on *all* in the upper room. Then Peter followed up with a masterful sermon about the Spirit being poured out on *all* people. Then *all* kinds of ordinary folks started flowing with the Spirit to make disciples, start ministries, and plant churches.

The beauty of the definition of multiplier is that everyone is called to it and anyone can do it. It is simple—not always easy, but simple. It is an "all skate" call that will give your life maximum Kingdom impact.

The Ripple Legacy of Multipliers

Few leaders tap into the exponential power of multiplication. Addition creates a big splash. You can easily see it. People go, "Wow!" Multiplication is not splashy or flashy. It creates no obvious splash. Multiplication ripples. It creates ever-expanding rings that quietly spread, creating larger and larger rings. It touches shores far from the original source. Those ripples go on after the stone has sunk.

As you read our book, you will encounter three overarching components in each chapter: 1) framework of our four seasons of life (based on Dr. Robert Clinton's work); 2) the life of Barnabas as a biblical guide; and 3) our lives and the lives of others as contemporary illustrations. We are so excited to share what we have learned as we adopted this framework to our life. We hope you will be encouraged by the "son of encourage-ment," as Barnabas has given us fuel for our journey. We pray you will learn key principles about how God shapes Kingdom multipliers over the course of a life. And we bless you with hope as you consider how God is shaping your life for maximum Kingdom impact and legacy.

SPRING

"Now 'tis spring, and weeds are shallow-rooted;
Suffer them now and they'll o'ergrow the garden."
–William Shakespeare

Grant and Miho Buccholtz are church planters in Tokyo, Japan. For the last 10 years they have planted and pastored Tokyo Life Church. I have had the joy of walking with them as they developed as planters, pastors, and parents. This past year, Becky and I met with Grant and Miho during Sakura season. *Sakura* is the Japanese word that means "cherry blossom." Once a year during spring, sprays of sakura burst forth from every street, park, temple, and outside Tokyo Life Church. The one million sakura trees, ranging from sand beige white to cotton candy pink, are a breath-taking spectacle for travelers from all over the world. For a few weeks every spring, the explosive colors literally make the entire city stop, stare, and take innumerable selfies.

Spring is the season in the calendar that is full of life. The days become longer, the temperatures climb, and yes, the flowers blossom. Spring is the season when nature awakes and flowers bloom. The comedian Robin Williams observed, "Spring is nature's way of saying, 'Let's party!'"

Most leaders experience the spring season in the first quarter of their lives. Our lives begin with God's sovereign choices for us. None of us chose our parents, brothers, or sisters. None of us met with God to discuss his choice on the matter (though some of us sure wish we could have had that discussion). Why did God start your life where you were born? Why weren't you born on another continent? Why were you born the year you were born? Why weren't you born 100 years earlier or later? Paul Simon considers these issues in his song, "Born at the Right Time." God's priority during this first season is laying the foundation for our future life and ministry. Often without our knowledge, God imparts values, personality, and basic skills through our family and first set of friendships. In his sovereign love he gives us previews of our destiny, tests the character he is building, and patiently guides us into our leadership commitment.

The data for Barnabas's spring season is Acts 1:1–5:11. Building upon his family foundations of Levitical priesthood, Barnabas is with his family in Jerusalem when the Holy Spirit is poured out at Pentecost. Barnabas is among the first Christian disciples who were devoted to the apostles' teaching, prayer, fellowship, and meals (2:42-47). His spring season conclusion event is being honored with a new name after proving faithful with his finances.

My spring season began as a non-Christian. God, full of grace upon grace, rescued me from prison and a deadly rip current before I became a Christian. After my leadership commitment, God grew my inner life as I fell in love with Jesus through his Word, prayer, fellowship, and meals. God built my character, testing me, to prove and improve my faith. For centuries, the Sakura blooms in Japan marked the beginning of new life. Under the blossoms, friends, families, and co-workers celebrate life together under the trees, admiring the colorful blossoms, eating, drinking, and making merry. But the blossoms only appear for a short time, falling quietly like snow. And before you know it, the Sakura season is over. My spring season ended when I left UCLA, the ministry where God called me to faith, to learn leadership at USC. In the next five chapters, we consider the first major development stage of Barnabas's life. Larry and I trust these multiplier development principles are part of your spring season as well.

Chapter 1

11 Minutes and the Drive-by Shooting

Multiplier Insight: Destiny

Barnabas: the All-Pro Lineman

I am a die-hard NFL football fan. We have two NFL teams in Los Angeles, but I don't follow either of them. My cousin was the defensive coordinator for the Dallas Cowboys for two years. In his first year they were the number 9 ranked defense. They improved to number 8 his second year. Our family rooted for the Dallas Cowboys for two years. For his improvement, he was fired. My mentor said that every pastor needs one hobby (not five). I can name the third-string running back on every NFL team without looking at a roster. Some might call that a problem. I call it my fantasy football hobby. When I think of Barnabas, I think of the NFL.

The apostle Paul is the superstar quarterback who has become a household name. Paul is the one who stars in all of the insurance commercials and sells food. But the NFL, like ministry, is all about teams. Paul's jersey sells out and fills the stands. Children line up for autographs and selfies. But where would the quarterback be without his best lineman? Barnabas

is not a household name. His jersey hangs on the wall of his
home office (and maybe his children's homes). If you saw him at
a coffee shop, you would know he was a player but not know his
name. He would be honored as a Hall of Fame at his position,
but he would remain unknown to the majority of society. Well,
it is time to shine the light on Barnabas, give him his flowers,
and introduce the world to the most underrated leader in the
entire Bible.

Luke: the Beloved Physician

To understand Barnabas, we must first grasp his unique relationship with Luke, the only author in the New Testament who
features him. The Gospel of Luke and the Acts of the apostles
were written by a gentile medical physician. The name *Luke*
occurs only three times in the New Testament (Colossians 4:14;
2 Timothy 4:11; Philemon 24). We know Luke is the author of
both books because they are addressed to the same person, a
man named Theophilus. We know from a close reading of Acts
(especially the first-person narrative beginning in Acts 16) that
the author was part of the missionary church planting team.
While there is much debate about Luke's background, I agree
with the scholars who start Luke's story in Antioch.

Antakya, in southern Turkey near the Syrian border, is the
ancient city of Antioch. This is where disciples of Jesus were
first called Christians (Acts 11:26). The city was marvelous,
luxurious, and drew elite people from all over the world. It
was divided into four quarters, based on race and culture. The
church plant began when two faithful disciples from Cyprus
and Cyrene opened their mouths and began to proclaim Jesus.
These were the first to preach to Gentiles (up to this point
the Gospel had only reached Hellenist Jews). This makes the
church at Antioch the first truly multi-ethnic church in the
New Testament. Once word spread to the Jerusalem church

that a Jewish-Gentile fellowship had broken out in Antioch, the apostles sent Barnabas (a native of Cyprus) to investigate this new Kingdom development. When Barnabas saw this new grace from God, he recruited a young minister named Paul, and for one year they taught God's Word, developed leaders, and built up the church at Antioch. By Acts 13:2, the Holy Spirit appointed the first multi-ethnic church staff team: Barnabas, Saul, Simeon, Manaen (a lifelong friend of Herod the Tetrarch), and a man named Lucius of Cyrene.

I imagine Lucius is the same faithful evangelist from Cyrene who first shared his faith in Antioch (Acts 11:20). Imagine the grace this man experienced sitting under the powerful Kingdom teaching of Barnabas and Saul. Imagine the awe that filled his heart when he saw healing, demonstrations of God's power, signs, and wonders performed by Barnabas and Saul. Imagine the joy that filled his heart as he became friends and ministry partners with Barnabas and Saul. I agree with the scholars who believe the evidence proves that Lucius of Cyrene is the author of Luke and Acts.

In first century literature, it was common for authors to write for themselves a small cameo role in their larger work. Great Hollywood directors have modified this practice into today's medium. Quentin Tarantino is Jimmie in *Pulp Fiction*; Martin Scorcese is John in *The Wolf of Wall Street*; George Lucas is a blue-faced Baron Papanoida in *Star Wars: Episode III*; David Lynch is a spice worker in *Dune*. I believe the Beloved Physician wanted his readers to know he was at a prayer meeting where God inaugurated church planting. *Lucius* is the formal Greek name for the common name *Luke*.

One massive implication of this discovery is the multicultural witness of the Gospel. I minister in the city of Compton. It is one of the few cities in the world that elicits a strong reaction every time it is mentioned. I once was on a call and gave my zip code. The agent on the other end immediately said, "I'm sorry." True story. I regularly hear from my fellas in the hood, "I don't want to check out the church. Christianity is a white man's religion." With joy in my heart and hope in my spirit, I fire back, "Did you know that one of the four Gospel authors was Black?" Cyrene is modern day Northern Africa. The most famous Cyrenian, Simon (the man who carried Jesus' cross in Mark 15) has long been depicted as a man with very dark skin. Luke—the Gentile physician, author, and future church planter—was Black. And without Luke's wisdom, hard work, and writing skills, we would never know Barnabas.

Sovereign Start: Cyprus, Real Estate, and Jerusalem

Barnabas was born and raised as a Jewish Levite on the island of Cyprus. Because he was a Levite, he was raised in a structured, perhaps even strict, Jewish tradition. His heritage of Hebrew faith must have been recognized, and welcomed, by the original apostles in Jerusalem. His firm grasp of Jewish traditions would prove to be a necessary base for the multicultural Gospel advances he would later interpret for the Jerusalem church. In his "sovereign start," we see God had already laid a foundation for who Barnabas would become and what he would do in the Kingdom of God.

Cyprus was an island of great strategic importance in the first century. From 22 BC it was under control of the Roman senate mainly for trade purposes. Cyprus was on the regional maritime hubs. This bustling environment exposed the young Barnabas to Roman culture, pagan religions, and many business relationships. Barnabas, raised in the strength of the Jewish heritage, possessed the super-rare combination of Hebrew faith and Gentile business culture. He had a global perspective, knew many cultures, and was able to network with lots of people.

Scholars believe that Barnabas was in the real estate profession. The biblical evidence is that he is closely linked to more than one property. This was rare in the first century. In the fourth chapter of Acts, Barnabas does not sell a home but a field. This is a commercial property, not a primary residence. He lays the profits of the sale at the feet of the apostles. The downtown Jerusalem property where Jesus met with his disciples and in-stituted the sacred communion meal on the last night belonged to Barnabas's sister, Mary (Acts 12:12). Luke writes, "the house of Mary, the mother of John." This was also where the 120 disciples gathered when the Holy Spirit filled the house at the Pentecost festival. In the first century, women were banned from owning property. Men were always mentioned before their wives in ancient literature. Luke not mentioning Mary's husband likely means that John Mark's father died early. I believe the home was owned by Barnabas and he lent it out to his sister for her and the ministry.

We do not know whether Barnabas moved to Jerusalem prior to Pentecost. J.A. Robertson suggests that he migrated to Jerusalem and became a ruler of his own synagogue. But that is highly debated. We do know that Barnabas had deep family roots in Jerusalem. His sister and nephew were among the very inner-circle of Jesus and the first disciples. His home was the community hub. Did Barnabas ever meet Jesus? While no mention is made of a personal encounter with the Living God, we know Barnabas was at the house on Pentecost. Was he there on the last night? How could he not respond to his sister's invite? His family ties to Jesus likely mean that he shared a bowl of hummus with the Word become flesh.

"Spring season" is the beginning of a person's lifelong ministry development. God is in complete control as he lays the foundation of family, values, environment, and development experiences. God is sovereign in every choice at the outset of our lives. The Father knew Barnabas would be his leader for a very important future ministry. Barnabas's Jewish tradition, exposure to Roman culture, commercial real estate background, and deep family roots in Jerusalem were all God's design. This pointed to a powerful ministry destiny: God's predetermined, irresistible future that he would bring to pass in the life of his disciples.

Mom's Prayers and the Drive-by Shooting

My spring season began in Hacienda Heights, a suburb 20 minutes east of downtown Los Angeles. My family never went to church growing up. My Korean mother was not religious. Because of bad missionaries in Seoul she actually disliked Christians. Our family suffered through a terrible accident, and my father died when I was 10 years old. By my teen years, things were so broken in my life that my mom turned to God and dedicated me to him. The Holy Spirit answered her prayers. Big time.

When I was a junior in high school, I was partying very late with my friends. My friend Jaxon (not his real name) was driving the car. Out of nowhere, I heard the Holy Spirit say to me, "Go, home!" Obviously this had never happened to me before. I thought it was the alcohol. But I heard the Spirit again, "Go, home!" I thought I should obey the voice. So I told my friends to drop me off. They made fun of me. But I insisted. I stumbled drunk into my home at 1 a.m., desperately trying to not wake my mom.

Court records show that at 1:11 a.m. a gun was discharged from a car into a truck on the CA 60 freeway at Azusa Avenue. After my friends dropped me off, they went to buy drugs. On the way to the drug dealer's house, a truck cut my friends off. Jaxon honked, flashed his lights, and swerved into the other lane. His dad's gun was stashed under his seat (I had no idea). In drunken anger, he discharged six rounds into the truck. Three bullets hit the driver in his legs. The driver was an off-duty police officer.

The next evening, Jaxon's incredibly accurate police sketch was the lead story on the news. Jaxon received a 12-year prison sentence for a freeway shooting. California law mandates that any passenger in a car in which a firearm is discharged is immediately sentenced to 7 years in prison. No exceptions. No negotiations. Straight to prison. My friend Ashton, the front passenger, was sentenced to 7 years. Breece (right rear seat) received 7 years. But my seat was empty. At 1:00 the Holy Spirit told me, "Go home!" When shots were fired 11 minutes later, I was in my bed. I missed 7 years in prison by 11 minutes. My Mom prayed to Jesus, "If you are real, will you please take care of John?" Jesus is really good at taking care of lost sons. Being rescued from prison is one of God's foundational graces in my spring season.

I was not yet a Christian, but I knew God rescued me for a special purpose.

Multiplier Insight: Destiny

Leaders who multiply trust God's destiny. God lays our foundation during the spring season. What are the foundational graces God has given you? What clues does this reveal about your destiny?

Chapter 2

The Sounds and Sights of Pentecost

Multiplier Insight: Leadership Commitment

The first mention of Barnabas in Scripture occurs in Acts 4:36. But like any good Netflix series, we know there is a backstory for every key character. A quick review of how the Church began is instructive as we move toward our formal introduction to Barnabas, the Levitical priest and commercial real estate agent from Cyprus.

Luke begins his second work just as he did his first. The Acts of the Apostles is written to a man named Theophilus. Luke uses the phrase "most excellent" (Luke 1:3) to address his intended reader. This phrase in first-century culture was reserved for high-standing individuals in government or business. Most scholars believe that Theophilus was a high-ranking government official and that Luke's other motive beside evangelism in writing this document was to free Paul from an unjust execution. Or could it be that Theophilus is the major donor who helped fund the early church planting movement? Perhaps he is a connection from Barnabas's real estate work?

After the resurrection, Jesus presents himself alive to his
core group of the first future church plant. He promised his
disciples that power would fill them and transform them into his
witnesses in Jerusalem, all of Judea, Samaria, and the ends of
the earth (Acts 1:8). This is the central thesis and provides the
structural outline for the entire book of Acts. The three mission
regions, Jerusalem-Judea, Samaria and ends of the earth each
have their own Pentecost. The outpouring of the Holy Spirit
moves from big to small: national festival in Jerusalem; to town
square in Samaria; to Cornelius' living room.

The First Core Group Meeting

My wife, Becky and I (John) have planted two churches. We
will never forget the first meeting for each church. Consider
the 120 gathered in the upper room of Mark's mother's house.
They must have been so conflicted with emotions: bursting
with joy that Jesus was alive, scared beyond measure that Jewish
authorities were breathing threats and murder, waiting with
hope for the promise of the Holy Spirit, heartbroken and angry
at the loss of their friend, the betrayer. This must have been a
brutal first church planting meeting. No amount of Chick-Fil-a
sandwiches could prepare the core group to discuss the two
agenda items: 1) process suicide and 2) replace Judas.

Peter stood up (Acts 1:15). He will stand up again to deliver his
first sermon (2:14). Every church planter will have moments
in their ministry when they must stand up. The first time Peter
stands, he shepherds the core group through the suicide of the
treasurer of the church plant. Peter masterfully uses the Book of
Psalms to guide his flock through profound pain. Bible-centered
leadership, especially the daily use of Psalms, is one of the
secrets of leaders who finish well. Peter holds no detail back
as he exposes Judas' greed and wickedness, delivering a vivid
description of his death. In moments of great transition, leaders

must be transparent and provide all appropriate details. From the Word, Peter brings closure and warning. The meeting is resolved as Matthias is appointed as an apostle.

I must share a quick leadership note on Judas. Dr. J. Robert Clinton, author of *The Making of a Leader*, identifies six traps (I like to call them spiritual pits) to finishing well: pride, power, family, finances, sex, and plateauing. We can never be too cautious or careful with our personal and ministry finances. At Jesus' anointing, Judas voices public frustration that Lazarus' sister's alabaster flask of pure nard oil was wasted. Perhaps he wanted the bag for himself to add to his second-home property fund. As my best friend Isaac Flores' faithful mother, Rachel, always taught him, "Mijo, your sins will find you out." Judas fell into the trap of financial greed. He betrayed the Living God. He bought a beach house. It all ended for him in suicide.

The Sounds and Sights of Pentecost

As we read familiar texts, it is easy to miss details. Because our study focuses on Barnabas, I read every section wondering about his development. We have established that the 120 are gathered in the Jerusalem home of Barnabas's sister. We are on solid footing to assume Barnabas is inside the home. He is Mary's brother. He is John Mark's cousin. He is a Levitical priest. And oh yeah, he owns the house. Was he chatting it up with James and John, the sons of Zebedee, before Peter stood up? He was one of those gathered together, unanimous in mind and action (Acts 2:1). God sent a sudden sound from heaven. Did Barnabas drop his drink when he heard the loud and confusing roar? This sonic boom from the next dimension of reality was so powerful and so arresting, conference attendees from every nation ran to the home (2:6). I doubt any of us has ever heard a sound this loud before in our lives. The city of Jerusalem would swell from the normal half a million people to

2.5 million during the Pentecost festival. The heavenly thunder clap drew everyone to Barnabas's home.

The Holy Spirit appealed to the unbelieving crowd through sound and sight. A divided tongue of fire rested on each of the disciples. There are six times in the Old Testament when God sends fire from heaven. The most famous event is when God vindicates Elijah in the power encounter against Jezebel's 450 false prophets (1 Kings 18:37). But this fire is different. The fire is contained and does not consume. The fire is public yet personal. The fire is symbolic yet prophetic. What a moment for Barnabas to look around and see a tongue of fire dancing and resting on his sister, his nephew, his friends! The fire did not injure anyone. The fire gave power to the disciples for witness. Charles Spurgeon reminds us, "Note that the emblem was not only a fire, but a tongue of fire. For God means to have a speaking Church." And speak they did!

The crowd could not believe their ears and eyes. The work of the Holy Spirit is always two-fold: God works in the witness, while simultaneously working in those who receive the word. The best example of this is the concurrent grace in Philip and the Ethiopian Eunuch (Acts 8:26-40). God not only empowers his Church to speak, but it is like he puts Kingdom translation devices in the ear of every hearer. Every person in the crowd is astonished, for they hear the heavenly tongue in *their* native language. The outpouring of the Holy Spirit to unify the world in Kingdom language is a reversal of the curse issued in Genesis 11. At Babel, God used language to separate and protect the ambitious from living a life without God. At Pentecost, God used language to unite and invite the world into a multiethnic family with God at the center. Glory!

We live in a world where the rich will pay incredible amounts of money for a trip to space. How much would the wealthy pay for the heavenly sounds and sights from Pentecost? The people were amazed and perplexed. The disciples must have been filled with so much joy. Every disciple had their own tongue of fire resting upon them. Well, almost every one. I cannot help but think of Judas. How short-sighted of him to desire money over the promises of God. What an absolutely horrible trade to choose a property over the tongues of fire. Judas is not only faithless, corrupt, and evil, but he is really stupid. He chose to purchase a dull and dim flashlight from Home Depot when he possessed the sun. His life was filled with darkness. His tongue of fire was given to someone else. The fleeting promises of sin never deliver.

Living Room Leadership Commitment

"Leadership committal" is the technical term that describes the moment when an emerging Christian leader chooses all-out surrender to Jesus. This commitment normally happens in the spring season, a special moment that tells God the leader is all in, with no looking back. I believe that at Pentecost, Barnabas committed everything to Jesus. The spiritual investment of his father and mother prepared him for a moment like this. All of his Levitical priesthood training was fulfilled. They were pieces of the larger puzzle. God wanted him in that house. God wanted him to hear the sound, see the fire, and speak of God's grace. What else would Barnabas want to do with his life? He didn't know what it all meant, but he knew God was real and worthy of everything.

Like Barnabas, I had a powerful encounter with the Holy Spirit in a house dedicated to ministry. When I was 22 years old, I made a commitment at UCLA to become a disciple of Jesus. I had no faith when I went to college, but I began attending a friend's dorm Bible study. Six months later I made a commitment to Jesus at a weekend college retreat. Five days after my conversion I was invited to a backyard church BBQ by my

friend (and now pastor) Adam Peacocke. The prayer meeting
was at the home of Pastor Ken Dew in Northridge, California.
After eating delicious chicken in the backyard, 30 UCLA
students piled into the living room for prayer and worship. I
had never been to church, so I didn't know any of the songs. I
had no idea Christian music was a thing. Things really started
getting interesting when Pastor Ken said, "It is now time to
prophesy." I felt a little uneasy. What did that mean? A man in
a sweat-stained French blue dress shirt (it was quite hot in May)
gave Pastor Ken a thumbs up. He was ready to tape the prophe-
cies. I figured I was a Christian now, so I should roll with it.

Pastor Ken was a large man from the South. His deep drawl
and hulking frame made me think he was a Georgia football
player. He had really kind eyes and a soft, strong voice. He
looked around at our group and then looked me in the eyes.
He said, "John, let's begin with you. Please stand up." Five days
earlier, I stood up alone to become a disciple. And now, my
knees buckled. I instinctively bowed my head. I snuck a peek at
Adam, who looked excited for me. I had never met the pastor
before, so he didn't know my story. But God used him to reveal
my destiny and secure my leadership commitment.

Pastor Ken began, "Thus, says the Lord: 'John, I love, forgive
you, and I have received your commitment.'" How could
he know that I became a disciple five days earlier? I started
weeping. Pastor Dew went next: "Thus says the Lord: 'John, I
will make you a teacher of my Word.'" I was stunned, astonished, and fired up for mission. On my way to the car, the man
in the sweat-stained French blue shirt gave me an audio tape
labeled with a Sharpie. It simply said: "John, May 13, 1992."
At 22 years old, I knew I belonged to God, and I committed to
serve him all my days.

Multiplier Insight: Leadership Commitment

Leaders who multiply understand their own leadership commitment. They are able to share it in passionate detail with those they lead. What were the circumstances in your spring years that brought you to submit to God? What lessons can you share with those you lead about your commitment to seek God first?

Chapter 3

The Basics Are Never Boring

Multiplier Insight: Inner Life

One out of three Christian leaders finishes well.

I first read that phrase in the book *The Making of a Leader* from Dr. J. Robert Clinton. But I truly understood that phrase in my first class with Clinton at Fuller Seminary. He began our 10-week course by asking three leaders to stand. I remember one leader was from Kenya, another from Korea, and the third leader was from the United States. Clinton stressed that finishing well means at least four things: 1) you have maintained a vibrant relationship with God; 2) your family (spouse and children or singles community) is healthy and intact; 3) you have finished the work the Father has given you to do; and 4) you have avoided the traps that disqualify. Clinton shared that from his voluminous research of 10,000 biblical, historical, and contemporary case studies, the data is downright depressing. He had the class look at each of the leaders who were standing. He asked us to consider their spouse, their children, their call, their ministry, their finances, and the people who depend upon them. It was quite a moment, really looking into our two brothers and one sister. With harsh abruptness and sudden severity, Dr. Clinton commanded, "Now, two of you sit down." The three leaders were confused, sheepish, and wondered whether they should sit down. Two sat down. One remained standing. It was a somber moment and bold illustration, but numbers don't lie.

If you are like Larry and me, you are sick and tired of hearing about leaders who do not finish well. Can we do more than sit back, bracing for impact when the next Christian leader cuts corners, chooses folly, and wrecks their ministry? We wrote this book to provide perspective, encouragement, hope, and a plan of action. There is one primary reason why two-thirds of leaders fall, quit, and do not fulfill their calling: the state of their inner life. The inner life of the Christian leader collapses long before the public fall. The spring season of development should overflow with inner-life growth. If you are going on a long drive, the first step is to make sure you have enough fuel. Inner life is the fuel that fills the Christian leader with God's love, truth, and wisdom. "Inner life" is the technical term that describes how God shapes our character, fills us with truth, and fuels us with intimacy. The Christian leader who ignores or puts off inner-life growth is playing with fire. They will eventually burn themselves.

The Fisherman's First Sermon

Peter stands up a second time in chapter two. I wonder what Peter's morning was like the day he preached his first sermon. Luke provides no details about what he ate, his route to Mary's home, or kissing his wife and children good-bye. But I can assure you that he did not have "preach first public sermon" and "exhort 3,000 international pilgrims to become disciples" on his to-do list. How could he know that the promise God made generations earlier through the prophet Joel would become reality that day? But God was sending the same Spirit who hovered over the formless void (Genesis 1:2). God was sending the same Spirit who led Israel through the desert as a cloud by day and a fire by night. God was sending the same Spirit who was in young David as he fell Goliath. God was sending the same Spirit who anointed Jesus to preach good news to the poor. But no one dared imagine it would be *this* good. No one could have predicted how personal and powerful the Pentecost promise of power would be inside each disciple.

We need not break down every part of Peter's sermon. Authors far more advanced than me have handled this text like a surgeon. But what I do not want us to miss is that God transformed a coward into a man of courage. A month earlier, this rugged fisherman from Galilee had denied Jesus three times. He could not tell the truth about his best friend to a preteen female servant. When she asked him, "Do you know Jesus?" he was afraid and lied. He broke down and wept at his seemingly incurable brokenness. But the Father forgave, healed, and strengthened Peter. Jesus filled Peter with the Holy Spirit. Peter became righteous and bold like a lion, publicly condemning the very same people who murdered Jesus (and wanted to do the same to him). Our God turns cowards into apostles.

Peter's first sermon was excellent. Luke tells us that the first hearers were cut to the heart. The Word of God had come alive and transformed their understanding of reality. When the Word goes out in power in Luke, the Beloved Physician repeats a phrase: "What must we do?" Seven times after the Word is preached, people plead with the preacher for guidance. Peter's answer echoes Jesus' first sermon, "Repent and believe in the Gospel." To repent means to literally "turn the other way." Imagine that right now you decide to drink a glass of water, but halfway to the kitchen, you decide against it. You return to your chair and finish this chapter. You have just repented from drinking a glass of water. *Repent* is a great word that in the original language does not carry with it emotionalism. To repent does not mean to feel guilty. Repentance is clearly turning away from something to go into another direction.

New Life, New Lifestyles

Some truly amazing miracles went down that morning. God sent a sonic boom from heaven. The Holy Spirit performed signs of sight and sound. Peter's sermon brought conviction and commitment to over 3,000 people. But might I be so bold to assert that none of these were the most excellent Pentecost miracle? The greatest miracle was that the 3,000 people went to a national conference, repented and were baptized, and never went home. Can you imagine attending a weekend conference but staying for three years because the Holy Spirit moved? That is what happened at Pentecost! What would possibly cause so many new believers to make such a dramatic life change? I believe the answer is God's love.

When we fall in love, our worlds are turned upside down. So it was at Pentecost. The first converts fell in love with God and with each other. They found what they had been searching for all their lives. They found their treasure in the field. They did not want to get back on a plane and go back to their old lives. Truth always brings transformation. New life in Jesus always produces a new lifestyle. And this new lifestyle is centered on four areas of life that completely transformed Barnabas:

1. Meals

Barnabas and the church were devoted to meals. Almost every culture in the world has food at the center of relationships, family, and celebration. Over a meal, you make new friends and deepen existing friendships. But the church eating with glad and generous hearts was far more than backyard cookouts, Korean BBQ, and shaved ice. Barnabas and the first disciples shared a theological meal together. Two months before the

Pentecost outpouring, Jesus established the holy sacrament
of communion. Barnabas embraced his own depravity as he
ate the bread broken for him. He rejoiced beyond measure in
knowing the new covenant was ratified by Jesus with his own
blood. He literally saw this happen with his own eyes. Barnabas
and his friends ate the meals believing that Christ could
return at any moment, making it the last time they enjoyed
communion. Barnabas and the church were devoted to meals.

2. Fellowship

Barnabas and the church were devoted to fellowship. God called
together 3,000 strangers to be family for each other. As the
Holy Spirit poured love into their hearts, they learned to love
one another. I can only imagine the friendships that formed.
They learned about each other's cultures. They asked questions
about "why they did things that way." They actively listened
with hearts full of love. The first church prioritized their new life
together over all things. I remember the first years of planting
the Fountain of Life Covenant Church. Becky and I hosted
a weekly life group Bible study. Dinner was served at 6:30,
and Bible study began at 7.30. Our small group of 20 people
bonded deeply. We shared our life stories. We joked around.
We played games. We laughed. The time literally flew by. One
night we fellowshipped so hard, we spilled into the driveway
and kicked it until the morning paper was delivered. People do
amazing things when they fall in love with God and each other.
Barnabas and the church were devoted to fellowship.

3. Prayer

Barnabas and the church were devoted to prayer. I can only
imagine the joy that filled the house where they prayed together.
Imagine the encouragement and conviction of those who saw
with their own eyes the Lord Jesus ascend into heaven. Imagine
the vibrancy of faith and the boldness of requests to the Father.
The church prayed for one another and for Christ's mission to
advance. While we might not have the same passion, personal

testimony, or dancing tongues of fire, our Father is the same God who sits on the same throne. We know that when we call on him in a day of trouble, he will rescue us (Psalm 50:15). As we struggle under spiritual challenges, coming together in prayer is our great reminder of the power God has given his people. Barnabas and the church were devoted to prayer.

4. Word

Barnabas and the church were devoted to the apostle's teaching. New life brings about a hunger for God's Word. New disciples must learn how to listen to, study, and live out God's Word. Consider that none of Jesus' ministry had yet been recorded. The new converts had little to no understanding of Jesus. But then Peter stood up and said, "He called me out of the boat, and I walked on water." Matthew took his turn and said, "Jesus taught me to begin praying with, 'Our Father who art in heaven.'" John set their souls on fire, teaching them that "the Word became flesh and dwelt among us." In our churches today, there are so many who lack proper training in the knowledge of God's Word. Like the first converts at Pentecost, they must be taught God's Word. They must learn to drink the good milk and then go on to graduate to the good meat (Hebrews 5:14). Barnabas and the church were devoted to the apostle's teaching.

In my own life, I have discovered a four-level equipping formula to master the Bible over the course of a lifetime. The first level is devotional: spending quality time with God in the Psalms. The second level is familial: reading larger books, sections, units, or even the entire Bible for a 30,000-foot information perspective. The third level is topical: studying key discipleship areas to have a strong grasp of truth on many matters. The fourth level is core: an in-depth manuscript study on a section or complete book of the Bible. My testimony is that as I have tried to master the Bible through core book study, the Bible has mastered me. For a detailed workbook to begin your own Bible mastery plan, please visit johnteter.org.

Multiplier Insight: Inner Life

Leaders who multiply understand the centrality of inner life. The basics are never boring. If a leader is not devoted, even addicted, they have not gone deep enough with Jesus.

Chapter 4

Barnabas and the Serpent-Vibes Couple

Multiplier Insight: Financial Obedience

The Negative Model of College Tennis Players

When I was 10 years old, my father died tragically in a glider plane accident. Losing my father at such a young age left a massive hole in my little world. One of the ways God filled that void was through tennis. My mother played tennis recreationally while she earned her masters in New York City. She passed her love for the game on to me. She provided an excellent coach who gave me weekly lessons at our local tennis center. I spent all my days playing tennis with friends. A few college players ran the pro shop and took me under their wings. (The head pro told them of my loss, and they went out of their way to help me.) Most of their influence was great, especially tennis, but some of it was very bad. They showed me how they stole from the hotel by not charging walk-ins. They pocketed cash (for beer) every shift. I was 14 years old. It left a lasting impression on me.

In the spring season of his life and ministry, Barnabas was disciplined in faith and finances. God knew Barnabas would be trusted with money down the road, so he discipled him early in this critical area. Christian leaders are tested early and often to be obedient in finances. Financial faithfulness is a theme in the early chapters of Acts. In chapter 1, we see that Judas is unfaithful with ill-gotten gain (Acts 1:18). In chapter 2, there is no need among the disciples because those with resources were faithful to give sacrificially (2:45). Have you ever wondered why Luke stresses that the early church had many with no need? I think it was because there was a very needy group among the first disciples. Thousands of international pilgrims stayed in Jerusalem and needed housing and basic supplies as they began their discipleship. I wonder if Barnabas used his real estate wisdom and background to help provide housing for 5,000 disciples over a three-year period. In chapter 3, Peter and John heal a man at the beautiful gate. When Peter is asked for money, he says that he has no silver or gold (3:6). Isn't it interesting that the senior pastor of a 3,000-person megachurch has no money? He has no money because he gave it all away to fund the basic needs of all the new disciples. How many megachurch pastors can say the same today? From the very beginning, the Father tested all the disciples, including Barnabas, early and often with his finances.

Barnabas, Satan, and the Disobedient Couple

It takes four chapters for us to finally meet Barnabas in Scripture, but wow, it is worth the wait! The Levitical islander emerges from the text as Exhibit A of Christian faithfulness in regard to obedience and finances. Barnabas was faithful with little by creating the church hub in his sister Mary's Jerusalem home. A few chapters later he is now faithful with much, creating many mission hubs for all the new disciples in the church (Luke 16:10). Barnabas is a man of great integrity. He is sensitive to the Holy Spirit. Therefore, he sacrificially gives to the "Jerusalem Discipleship-Dorm Fund." When Barnabas sells his field and presents the check at the feet of the apostles, we see a joyful obedience. Luke emphasizes how Barnabas is among those who are of "one heart and mind" with the Holy Spirit. There is not one trace of self-protection, doubt, or deceit when Barnabas puts his field on Zillow and sells it for the Kingdom.

The word *field* introduces three contrasts to Barnabas's great gift. The first time the word *field* is mentioned in the Bible, it is where Cain killed his brother Abel (Genesis 4:8). Then Judas, the betrayer, bought a field with the reward of his wickedness (Acts 1:18). He died in the middle of that same field, with his bowels bursting and gushing out of his body. It is hard to think of a worse death. His reward for sinful wickedness is an eternity in hell. But Barnabas chooses life. Instead of buying a field with blood money, Barnabas joyfully sells his field and gives clean money to the Kingdom mission. Judas bought a field and died. Barnabas gave a field, and boy, did he live!

The third contrast is Barnabas set against a couple named Ananias and Sapphira. We know that Luke contrasts this couple with Barnabas because the accounts are placed next to each other. As we begin Acts 5, the community of faith is really beautiful. Everyone is of one accord, fully unified around the vision of discipleship dorms, except for Ananias and Sapphira. The irony is that they are not hardened, defiant, or violent, but they teach us a valuable lesson: partial obedience is never enough. They sell a piece of property, but they hold back some of the profit for themselves. Satan fills the heart of Ananias to do this, and his wife agrees (Acts 5:3). A man and woman being lured into disobedience by Satan gives off serious Adam and Eve vibes. If Ananias and Sapphira function as a New Testament Adam and Eve, then wealth and possessions are the New Testament apple. They bit the apple and died. Jay-Z warns us in "Empire State of Mind:" "Lined with casualties who sip life casually, then gradually become worse, don't bite the apple, Eve!"

I agree with D. M. Lloyd-Jones, who argues that no account in Acts has provoked more wrath from critics than the story of this disobedient couple. Commentators have complained about the difficulty of accepting the death of both husband and wife in Peter's church office. They have questioned Peter's ethics in not giving them an opportunity for repentance and in not telling Sapphira of her husband's death. I admit, this passage is hard to read. In our current world of human resources and social media, a man and wife dying on the same day while meeting separately with the pastor, is a public relations nightmare. I can only imagine Peter being interviewed in the church parking lot telling a reporter, "You see, the Lord killed the husband and wife for their disobedience." The internet would literally melt down. Peter would immediately be locked up and sent to prison.

But these critics miss the point. Luke closes his account of Ananias and Sapphira's sin and consequences with the summary statement "Great fear came upon the whole church and upon all who heard of these things" (Acts 5:11). This is a vignette of warning. Luke is only following God's leadership to stress this note of reverent fear. Allen Iverson is famous for his tattoo: "Only God can judge me!" There is a defiant note, as if not being judged by people is the goal. I want to shout from the rooftops to the unbelieving world: "God will judge you!" The Lord takes financial obedience very seriously. When we begin to lie, we play the same game of the evil one. The devil was a liar and murderer from the beginning (John 8:44). We can never be too transparent or too careful with our personal and ministry finances. He wants to trust us with current, and future, Kingdom finances. This is why God tests our financial obedience early and often.

Obedience Testing Patterns

Did you know that God tests his leaders? He tested Abraham with Isaac. For those who missed the season finale, Abraham did not bring a rubber knife (Genesis 22:16). David was tested with Bathsheba. After he fell into sexual immorality and murder, David's family and personal life never recovered (2 Samuel 12:9). God forgave David, but he was tormented with the consequences of his sin for the rest of his life. His leadership plummeted, and he died in the arms of a prostitute (1 Kings 1:2). Daniel was tested when he was 81 years old and embraced all the personal sanctions and persecution for praying to Israel's God. The traditional pit of lions was a 12-foot drop. I imagine that Daniel never walked again after that fall (Daniel 6:20). In the New Testament, John tells us that Jesus tested Philip by asking what the plan was regarding the hungry seekers. Philip responded with a snark and sass, "Should we go to Jersey Mike's and buy $60,000 worth of sandwiches?" Jesus prayed and multiplied five barley loaves into 5,000 delicious meals (John 6:11).

God tests his leaders to prove and improve our faith. "Obedience testing" is the technical term that describes how God teaches a leader to learn obedience. A positive response to the test is usually followed by a deepening of character and an expansion of ministry ceiling. A negative response to the test is usually followed by remedial training. The young leader enters into a season, often without knowing it, where God personally works on that discipleship area until the next test on the same material. In my own life, God has tested me on finances early and often. Below are two accounts of God calling me to obedience in my finances. I bombed the first test. I passed the second test. God is full of grace upon grace.

Even My Favorite Hoodie?

USC recently defeated UCLA on a cold, misty night at the Los Angeles Memorial Coliseum. The game for LA bragging rights made me think of my all-time favorite sweatshirt: my thick but cozy, embroidered (not pressed), perfectly fitting college hoodie. I grew up in the suburbs of Los Angeles, so I was never exposed to poverty. But when I became a Christian, I quickly learned of God's love for the poor. His clear command is to join him in loving those on the margins. Jesus teaches that the surest sign that you believe in the resurrection is that your life is filled with loving people who can never pay you back (Luke 14:14). In my first year of discipleship, I was pumping gas one late night in November. I met a homeless man at the gas station. He walked up to my car and asked me for help. He was cold (even by Los Angeles standards). He was only wearing a T-shirt. His right elbow was so full of fluid, it looked like a softball somehow slipped under his skin. He was in bad shape. My guy really needed help. God brought him to me. He was testing the Kingdom values I was learning in Bible study. Would I love this man?

I sensed the Holy Spirit impressing on me, "John, give him your sweatshirt." Instead, I bought him food in the gas mart. God's still, small voice spoke again, "John, give him your sweatshirt." Instead, I asked him if he needed a ride. As we drove to his spot, I knew I was supposed to give him my sweatshirt. But I negotiated with myself, "This is my only sweatshirt with a hoodie." As we pulled up to his destination, I heard God speak to me in a gentle but firm voice, "John, give him your sweatshirt." Instead, I chose disobedience. My guy left my car, with his giant right elbow, into the cold night.

I failed my test. But God worked with me. Later that year, I had my second Kingdom economics test.

"John, You Are the Tax Collector."

On the day I turned 18, I was hired by a hotel to teach youth tennis and run the pro shop. As a boy I longed for the day when I could be like the college tennis players. Unfortunately, I chose to follow the model of stealing court fees from the hotel. I pocketed walk-in charges for almost two years. In my second year of discipleship, I studied Zaccheus the tax collector coming to faith (Luke 19:1-10). The Holy Spirit convicted me with the simple phrase, "John, you are the tax collector." God was calling me to financial restitution. In faith, I made an appointment with my former boss. I withdrew $3,000 from my account to give back to the hotel. She was blown away that I would do this. Our meeting ended with her confession that she was an alcoholic. She asked me to pray for her. She said she would give the money to the hotel.

A few days later, the hotel general manager called me for a meeting. Stealing over $499 is a felony in California. As I prepared for the meeting, I was certain I would be arrested. (I even wore my glasses, not my contact lenses, in case I had to spend the night in prison.) But God delivered me. I boldly proclaimed Jesus to the general manager, who did not call the police. He said he would donate the money to charity. God did not call me to prison ministry. And more importantly, I passed my financial restitution obedience test.

Multiplier Insight: Financial Obedience

Leaders who multiply understand that God will test his leaders for financial obedience early and often. They should expect this in the spring season. We are called to earn, save, give, and make right all past financial wrongs. When we pass our tests, God will expand ministry. Barnabas aced his exam. Have you passed your financial obedience tests?

Chapter 5

Gifts, Names, and Leader Expectations

Multiplier Insight: Spiritual Gifts

The First Bible Study I Ever Led

The first time Luke introduces Barnabas, he does so in the context of spiritual gifts. Barnabas was known in the Jerusalem church for two things: encouragement and generosity. In this spring season of his life and ministry, his gifts are already quite developed. This got me all nostalgic as I asked myself when I first used one of my spiritual gifts.

As I wrote in chapter 2, I became a Christian in May the year I turned 22. Five days into my discipleship I received a prophetic promise, "I will make you a teacher of my Word." The next month I went on a retreat and inductively studied Mark 1:1–8:31. I fell in love with God's Word. My life was changed forever. But I still had the summer before I returned to UCLA, so I met with all my friends to share my new-found faith in Christ. My friends were all worldly partiers. I thought they would all be so happy and want to become a disciple just like me. A few were excited and open. Most were skeptical and guarded. Some were mad and closed. But all were curious about what in the world happened to me. So I decided to recreate the same environment of my own conversion. I secured the location. I made some flyers. I even cut up fruit (though my mom did most of the work). I was determined to lead my first Bible study at my friend's party house. (His Friday night house parties sometimes hit 500 people.) The study would be on a Saturday at noon, so everyone would be awake and not too hung over. I was locked in.

I drove to the Bible study with pens, clipboards, two plates of cut-up fruit, and 30 copies of Mark 4:1-20. Most of my friends were still there from the Friday night party. A few were still sleeping. But by 12:15, 22 people gathered around the Word. Most of them were sober, but a few had been up all night snorting cocaine. They were excited (in a jittery sort of way) for Bible study.

I explained the inductive method of Bible study. I told them that I was a facilitator. I encouraged them to find the answers to their questions in the text. I opened up in prayer. We read the text. The questions started coming at me fast.

"Is God real?"
"Is this Bible stuff true?"
"Isn't God just a giant buzz-kill?"
"What happened to you to make you all religious?"

I tried to nod in agreement to the questions like I saw my dorm Bible-study leader model for me. I calmly explained that we were going to look at the text and save the outside-the-text questions for after study, during snacks. The first question from the text came from Norm:

"Why did Jesus teach in parabolas?"

My friends got all over poor Norm. They called him a Bible dummy. They wondered how Norm could not know the difference between a parable and a parabola? My friend who had just snorted a line of coke before the study called Norm an idiot. You can't make this up.

The study was bad. The ending was a disaster. I finally hit my friends with the big question: "There are four soil types. Rocky is hard. Shallow is temporary. Thorny is worldly. Good soil bears a hundredfold fruit. So which soil type are you?" I expected everyone to break down crying and pray for God to transform them into fourth-soil disciples. But Susan raised her hand and said, "John, you are all high and mighty now! I am third soil. I am worldly. And I love it. You can't do anything about it." Others nodded in agreement. I looked around and finally said, "That's great. Let's wrap things up. How about I close us in prayer?"

When I got home, my mom asked me how my first Bible study went. (She really wanted to know if they liked the fruit.) I told her I learned a lot—and that I really needed to pray for my friends. My mom, who had not yet converted to Christ, told me she was proud of me. My mom was the best! God the Father was also proud of me, and happy for my growth. I had no idea that I was using three spiritual gifts. Without realizing it, I was putting into action apostleship, teaching, and evangelism. (These are my primary spiritual gifts that I still work to develop 33 years later.)

Author's Note: For the record, there were a few second-soil commitments, but nothing lasted. Over the years, I have noticed a few friends called me for help when their lives fell apart. One person who benefited from my first Bible study that summer was Jeff Hanson. Jeff is my friend from first grade. Today he is my lifelong friend and our best ministry partner.

Barnabas and Two Emerging Spiritual Gifts

There are 19 spiritual gifts listed in the New Testament. Our technical definition of a spiritual gift is a "God-given unique capacity that is given to a believer for the purpose of releasing a Holy Spirit-empowered ministry." Drs. J. Robert Clinton and Richard Clinton, in their excellent book *Unlocking Your Giftedness*, observe three categories in which the 19 gifts operate: word, power, and love. Drawing on the two parables Jesus taught on gifts (Matthew 25:14-30; Luke 19:27), the Clintons exhort Christian leaders to not only identify their spiritual gifts, but to do the much harder work of intentionally developing those gifts.

No one would argue that ministry builds up the Church. But leaders who effectively multiply know that ministry is also for personal development. In our spring season, we must approach our spiritual gifts with a developmental mindset. The more ministry we do, especially with an intentional learning posture, the more data we have for our unique spiritual gifts set. In the spring season, young leaders should say yes to every ministry opportunity. Yes, we are servants. But also, we don't know what we are good at yet. As we do real-world ministry, we will know (rather quickly for good or bad) if a spiritual gift is present and active. Your spiritual gifts should be identified, developed, and fully operational by the time you reach your autumn season. Spiritual gifts are a big part of every Christian leader's guidance and ministry future.

From Luke's account, it is clear that Barnabas operated in at least two spiritual gifts: giving and exhortation. As a founding member of the Jerusalem church, he was in a perfect community to learn and develop his gifts. The technical definition for the spiritual gift of giving is "the desire and means to give liberally to meet the needs of others and yet to do so with a purity of motive that senses that the giving is a simple sharing of what God has given." Barnabas likely learned to give of his resources by being under the leadership of Peter and John. We already established that these men did not have silver or gold (Acts 3:6). They were faithful givers, obeying Jesus' teachings on money, wealth, and possessions. Seeing these selfless leaders apply God's Word was likely such a stark contrast to those in the commercial real estate field he left behind. As we will see in Barnabas's summer season, he passed on the same value of giving Kingdom resources to those he discipled at Antioch (Acts 11:29). In his spring season, Barnabas identified and developed the spiritual gift of giving.

God also gave Barnabas the opportunity to develop the exhortation gift. Our technical definition of the spiritual gift of exhortation is "the capacity to urge people to action in terms of applying Biblical truths, to encourage people generally with biblical truths, or to comfort people through the application of Biblical truth to their needs." I like this definition because it identifies two poles and one center of gift usage. On one end of the exhortation spectrum, we have the admonisher. This person is likely intense, direct, hard-hitting, and expects instant response. John the Baptist operates in exhortation with an admonishing wing. A fine example of this, his first recorded exhortation is, "You brood of vipers! Who warned you to flee from the wrath to come?" (Luke 3:7). Hard-hitting indeed. In the middle of the exhortation continuum is the disciple who is wise, fair, and has no problem giving a call to action. I think of the apostle John and his mysterious, artistic, and symbolic teaching style. The opposite of the admonition bent is the comforter. This is the type of leader who oozes joy, always cheers up the room, and makes people want to follow Jesus because they are happy around them. Barnabas is the encouraging exhorter. In his spring season, Barnabas identified and developed the spiritual gift of exhortation.

The Power of Mentors (and Names)

We learn from this passage that the Levitical priest from Cyprus
was originally named Joseph. The apostles, for the first time
in their leadership development arc, change someone's name.
They are now doing Father and Son things, as three of the
original apostles had their names changed by Jesus (Mark
3:16-19). The name *Barnabas* means "son of encouragement."
The apostles gave him this name because he encouraged them,
and the entire Jerusalem church. Being given this name by the
men who walked with Jesus must have been utterly life-trans-
forming for Joseph.

The apostles in Jerusalem were so moved by his character, his
faith, and his person that they wanted to call out even more.
Recognizing his potential, Barnabas and his spiritual gift were
singled out from among the thousands of faithful disciples.

This is a fine example of the Goodwin Expectation Principle.
The thesis of this master teacher is this: "Almost always
followers will live up to, and even exceed, the genuine expectations of a leader he/she respects." When the apostles gave
Joseph a new name, they gave Barnabas the expectation that
his character had transformed. He was beginning a new season
of his life. When the apostles gave Joseph a new name, they
powerfully communicated that they saw his potential. When
the apostles gave Joseph a new name, they took on the some-
times-risky role of sponsoring a new leader's growing ministry
among the Jerusalem church. When the apostles gave Joseph a
new name, they focused on his great qualities (and his spiritual
gifting) to bring out the very best in him. And when the apostles
gave Joseph a new name, they raised his status and welcomed
him into a growing ministry network. When the apostles
changed Joseph's name to Barnabas, they laid the foundation
for the important ministry he would carry out in his summer,

autumn, and winter seasons. The apostles were such excellent mentors for Joseph. They taught, trained, modeled, and raised the Kingdom standards for their emerging leader. Renaming him Barnabas in front of the entire church not only encouraged him, but it paved the way for future leadership.

Multiplier Insight: Spiritual Gifts

Leaders who multiply understand that spiritual gifts are a key part of mentoring and leadership multiplication. The gifts emerge best in the context of a developmental ministry community.

Barnabas left his spring season aware of his destiny, committed to Kingdom leadership, devoted to the basics, passing his financial obedience exam, and with a new name.

Barnabas smashed his spring season. In his summer season, the Holy Spirit would bring into his life a young, troubled, violent, religious zealot named Saul.

SUMMER

Summer was another name for opportunity.
— *Maya Angelou*, I Know Why the Caged Bird Sings

Most leaders experience their summer season somewhere
between the ages of 25 and 45. My (Larry) summer season
started early. Perhaps because in my spring, I had committed to
Jesus at age 8, was baptized at 10, responded to a clear call to
full-time ministry when I was 12, had a powerful encounter with
the Holy Spirit when I was 15, and went to a Christian university to study for the ministry when I was 18. My spring revealed a
passionate desire to reach people for Jesus in any way possible.

By age 25, my summer season was kicking off. I was leading
youth ministries at the largest church in Seattle. The pastor
then started having me preach occasionally at our huge Sunday
evening service … heady stuff for a 26-year-old farm kid.
Summer would shape me, stretch me, and launch me into
unexpected levels of fruitfulness. My first lead pastor role, at
age 33, saw our church grow from a handful of folks to the
fastest-growing church in our denomination.

Summer, however, also brought some bad thunderstorms that
almost washed me away. The megachurch where I was youth
pastor fell completely apart. My marriage nearly fell apart as
well. I was deceived for a time in a doctrinal error. I tried to start
a non-profit. Summer can have tough times.

Agriculturally, summer is when the seeds that were planted in a
leader's spring begin to become visible. They stretch, grow, and
begin to bear fruit. Zucchini plants try to conquer my garden.

Summer is hot, bright, and demanding. Long days with short nights produce rapid growth and quick pace. Summer's hot sun either matures the young plants or shrivels them up. Summer is an exciting time as fruit visibly enlarges day by day. Summer is an apt metaphor for this stage in a leader's development.

Barnabas had a summer season that stretched from Acts 5:12 to 12:25. Under the training of the apostles at Jerusalem, Barnabas sprouts up as a wise and trusted leader. He steps into unfamiliar opportunities, navigates complex relationships, and follows God's leading with faith. He advocates for Saul when others distrust him, discerns grace at work in Antioch, teaches new believers for a full year (establishing one of the most vital churches of the first century), forms a mission team with Saul, and carries benevolence to those facing famine. Barnabas experienced the essence of summer: growing your gifts, courage, character, and fruitfulness.

For multipliers this season is also learning how to form partnerships, empower others, share your ministry platform, and encourage others to their highest potential. Barnabas models this powerfully—he seeks out Saul to help him lead the church in Antioch, shares teaching for a year, and joins in the plurality of elders at Antioch. His leadership development skills are growing. He is seeking the expansion of the Kingdom above increasing his own prominence.

In the next five chapters we learn five key multiplier insights from this summer season in Barnabas's life. These truths can shape us into multipliers as well.

Chapter 6

Jumping Out of Planes—and Other Sources of Power

Multiplier Insight: Empowerment

Multipliers seek increasingly empowered spiritual lives.

Recently I have given more thought to what I want engraved on the headstone of my grave. I am not sure whether it is copacetic for me to preselect nice words about me. It smacks of arrogance. Usually, those engravings are chosen by your closest family or friends, based on their knowledge of your life. Honestly, in my line of work, I have seen some big lies etched into the granite at grave sites.

Barnabas could honestly have had an awesome headstone. Luke, author of Acts, was probably giving his personal, first-hand assessment and also quoting those who knew Barnabas well when he summarized Barnabas's life in Acts 11:24:

"He was a good man, full of the Holy Spirit and of faith. And a great many people were added to the Lord."

This is the defining statement of Barnabas's life. God captures in his eternal Word a testimony to man who is largely ignored by Christian leaders. So much life and power in one sentence. I hope to live in such a way to have a similar epithet. How about you?

Within this summary of his life, we see four power sources that made Barnabas so fruitful: character, Spirit-fullness, faith, and mission focus. These same sources are what we must prioritize and pursue if we want to live as effective multipliers.

CHARACTER

Barnabas was a "good" man—morally upright; pleasing to God in his motives, words, and deeds; consistent between his private and public life. In its earliest use, the word *character* described something engraved into stone or metal, something lasting—not easily erased. Over time, this metaphor transformed into describing the engraved qualities of a person, the inner marks that define them. In Jeremiah 31:33, God promises to write his law on our hearts. Character is not something we know or outwardly do; it is something we are from the inside out.

Character over charisma: Our culture is prioritizing charisma like never before. Influencers and preachers can all look "good" from a distance, but you can only know that they are truly good when you get up close.

Power without character: There were once seven Jewish brothers who thought they could have power without character. They decided to use the name of Jesus as an "abracadabra" to evict demons from people. Their plan worked. They seemed to have ghostbusting power, until one day a particularly formidable demon blew their cover and asked "Who are you?" The demon then overpowered all seven of them and stripped them down. They fled naked. Their inner truth was revealed. They sought power without clothing themselves in Christ. It ended quite badly (Acts 19:13-18).

The Power Fruit

Character is not a surface trait. It's engraved through decisions, discipline, devotion, pressures, and vulnerability. Do not misunderstand, however; it is also the work of the Spirit.

When we think of empowerment, our minds rush to the gifts of the Spirit and the manifestations of the Spirit through our ministries. Instead, empowerment must prioritize sinking the *roots* of our lives deeper into Christ so that the *fruit* of the Spirit is produced in our lives.

Barnabas was a good man because one of the fruits of the Spirit is goodness, and he was full of the Spirit. The starting place for a definition of Christian character is Galatians 5:22-23: "But the fruit of the Spirit is love, joy, peace, patience, kindness, goodness, faithfulness, gentleness, self-control …".

How many Christian leaders want to be known for their love, patience, kindness, gentleness, faithfulness, or self-control? Those traits don't gather followers on social media.

Near the end of my summer season, I did my doctoral research project on the characteristics of effective pastors. I led a group of the leading pastors in America through a process of defining the most essential characteristics for a pastor. We produced a list of characteristics that became the *15 Characteristics of Effective Pastors*, published by Baker (co-authored with Kevin Mannoia). Out of the 15 characteristics, only 3 were skill-based, and the rest were character-based. After nearly 50 years in ministry, I have seen the truth of this research affirmed countless times. Character counts most over the long term.

One of Jesus' strongest statements in his greatest sermon is aimed at those who prioritize gifts over fruit, activity over identity. He declares that demon-slaying, future-telling, powerful sermons, and supernatural acts using his name will all end up being inadequate for kingdom entrance. Knowing him personally and taking on his character are essential (Matthew 7:21-23).

Paul echoes this in 1 Corinthians 13 when he identifies love as being the trait that outweighs gifts, miracles, and even martyrdom. In Ephesians 3, he goes to great lengths to link love and power together. Power comes when we receive deeply and distribute generously the love of God.

The deeper this kind of character is engraved in your heart, the greater source of power it becomes to your life and ministry, and the more effective your disciple-making and multiplication will be.

SPIRIT-FULLNESS

What's the most meaningful affirmation you have ever received? What is one of the highest commendations you read in the Bible? I would suggest this phrase about Barnabas captures it: "full of the Holy Spirit." John's description of Jesus was: "he whom God has sent utters the words of God, for he gives the Spirit without measure" (John 3:34).

Is the dove on your shoulder? John has a unique description of the Spirit descending on Jesus: "I saw the Spirit come down from heaven as a dove and remain on him." Strange, right? Is John giving us a picture of Jesus walking around with a dove cooing in his ear? Of course not. But he is telling us that Jesus lived a continually empowered life because he was yielded to the Spirit.

Barnabas was most likely filled with the Spirit on the day of Pentecost, but he refused to settle for an initial encounter with the Spirit. He sought the Spirit's power daily. He lived deeply dependent upon the Spirit's presence and power. The dove was on his shoulder.

It is a long shot, but it's possible that Barnabas, in mentoring Paul, taught him the truth of Ephesians 5:18: "Be filled with the Spirit." This phrase is in the present tense, imperative mood, and passive voice. This is important for multipliers. Present tense means "Keep on being." Imperative mood signifies "This is essential, not optional." Passive voice declares "Receive this filling because you can't fill yourself."

As soon as I realize I am awake for a new day, my first prayer is, "Holy Spirit, fill me fresh today!" Throughout the day I breathe this prayer, "Spirit, fill me now." The older I get (remember I am in winter) the more desperately dependent on the Spirit I realize I am.

Desperation seems like a terrible way to live, but it depends on who or what you are desperate for. If it's the Spirit who is sufficient for all my needs, always available and more desirous to give than I am to receive, then desperation is a delightful place of empowerment. This is where multipliers live.

This Spirit-fullness empowers us to hear the voice of God, grow spiritual fruit, exercise spiritual gifts, see miracles happen, perceive where the Spirit is already working, discern spiritual opposition, teach the Word, identify new disciples and church planters, and much more. Each of these manifestations of the Spirit flowed through Barnabas, the patron saint of ordinary folks who want to be multipliers.

FAITH

"Full of the Holy Spirit and of faith" … Barnabas was not just faithful to the end. He was full of faith until the end! His faith powered him through every situation, and people noted it.

Faith is an active trust in an unchanging God. Faith is taking action as if God is going to take action. Faith is personal confidence in God's immutable Word.

Our faith is only as empowering as the power and permanence of the object it is placed in. Too many leaders today are deceived into trying to put faith in their faith. They wrongly imagine, "If I have adequate faith, then God will empower me." John Stott corrects this thinking by explaining, "The promises of God are the foundation on which faith rests. Faith looks not at itself, but at Him who promises."[11]

I remember placing my faith in a mere 7 pounds of silk fabric called a parachute. My faith caused me to jump out of the plane from several thousand feet above planet Earth. But I did not scream, "I believe, I believe!" all the way down (although I may have shouted "Jesus, save" a few times!"). My confidence was in a trustworthy source, not myself. My super power was the parachute. I activated it by jumping. The quick trip to Earth was thrilling. I am happy to report that it finished quite well.

Barnabas "jumped" when he sold his property and gave it all to the mission. He "jumped" when he dared to befriend the Christian hunter, Saul, and bring him to the apostles. Over and over, we see Barnabas "jump" because he was full of faith. That's what multipliers do. This trait empowers their lives to do what most leaders will never do.

---

[11] John Stott, *The Message of 2 Timothy*, IVP, 1973, p. 49

Where did Barnabas's great faith come from? No doubt one of the primary sources was the Word of God itself. Growing up in Cyprus, a Levite boy like Barnabas would have learned Hebrew, memorized significant portions of the Torah, and participated in synagogue readings and discussions. Most Diaspora synagogues placed heavy emphasis on reading, memorizing, and discussing the Scriptures—especially among Levite families.

Then Barnabas spent at least a decade in Jerusalem after Pentecost, hanging out with the apostles who had walked with Jesus. The words of Jesus, while not yet formally gathered into the Gospels, were being quoted continuously. Barnabas would go on to spend a year teaching the Word in order to build one of the greatest churches in the first century: Antioch.

Barnabas loved the Word of God. His faith took its unwavering stand on God's truth and promises. He followed the direction the Lord gave to Joshua: "This Book of the Law shall not depart from your mouth, but you shall meditate on it day and night, so that you may be careful to do according to all that is written in it" (Joshua 1:8). Church tradition (probably embellished, but not hard to believe) says Barnabas was buried holding a copy of Matthew's Gospel.

Multipliers make the Word of God their life. They eat it as their daily bread. They view it as alive and active. They receive it as a daily love letter from their Father. Teaching their disciples to love and live the Word is a top priority. It feeds their faith.

Greg is a 67-year-old successful contractor I've been discipling. On the phone today, Greg exclaimed, "Man, the Bible has come alive to me. I'm telling people all the time, 'This book works!'" Indeed, it does. Faith arising from the Word is empowering!

MISSION FOCUS

"And a great many people were added to the Lord" (Acts 11:24).

This brief phrase about Barnabas's fruitfulness tells us much about his vision and passion in life and ministry. He focused his life on the mission of seeing people come to know Jesus. Focus empowers us.

John Wesley's impact as a multiplier was fueled by his laser focus. He lived by the exhortation he continually gave to his leaders: "You have nothing to do but to save souls. Therefore, spend and be spent in this work."[12]

Recent research on the state of pastors found that "pastors today are carrying too many roles, too many pressures, and too many expectations. The lack of focus significantly diminishes both their effectiveness and well-being."[13] Thom Rainier and Eric Geiger were even more direct: "The number-one reason pastors plateau in effectiveness is that they attempt to do too many things rather than focus on a few essential priorities."[14] Sadly the prevailing model of ministry in America demands that pastors wear many hats while spinning several plates.

But the way of Jesus was simpler, doable, sustainable, and focused. Jesus modeled this power with stunning simplicity. He described his entire earthly assignment in a single sentence: "The Son of Man came to seek and to save the lost" (Luke 19:10). Barnabas followed his example. His one thing was to

---

[12] John Wesley, *The Minutes of the Methodist Conferences, from the First Held in 1744*, vol. 1 (London: John Mason, 1862), 147.

[13] Barna Group, *The State of Pastors: Leading in Complexity*, Barna Group Research Report (Ventura, CA: Barna Group, 2022), 14.

[14] Thom S. Rainer and Eric Geiger, *Simple Church: Returning to God's Process for Making Disciples* (Nashville: B&H Publishing, 2006), 67.

advance the Gospel by empowering others. His mission focus fueled his effectiveness.

When I speak at pastor conferences I ask pastors to "tell me the names of the people you are personally discipling." The vast majority of them start to stutter. They aren't doing it. When I ask them, "Why aren't we majoring in what Jesus declared was the main thing?" The number one answer I get is, "We are too busy" or "We don't have time."

Yet, Warren Bird and Ed Stetzer's research concluded that "the most effective leaders relentlessly focus on the high-impact activities that multiply disciples."[15] Perhaps the reason our leadership is low on power is that we have little mission focus on what matters most.

Multiplier Insight: Empowerment

Leaders who multiply prioritize this empowerment. The good news is that the power Barnabas demonstrated in his life is available to every Christian. We, however, have been deceived into accepting our status quo empowerment level as "normal," as "the best we can expect." Ezekiel 47 shows a different way. We are satisfied with trickle power, ankle-deep power, knee-deep power, waist-deep power. But the power of the river is only fully experienced when we can no longer touch bottom, when we are in over our heads, and when it's the river that is carrying us. In Ezekiel's vision, that place of Spirit-reliance is where you find the fruit and fish in abundance (47:6-12).

---

[15] Warren Bird and Ed Stetzer, *Viral Churches: Helping Church Planters Become Movement Makers* (San Francisco: Jossey-Bass, 2010), 45.

Chapter 7

5 for 5 Ministry

Multiplier Insight: Empowering

Multipliers prioritize using the power of the Spirit to empower others.

Fourteen drowsy farmers and their somewhat more-alert wives sat scattered throughout the small sanctuary of First Church as I preached my first sermon. One especially exhausted farmhand snored loudly with his head tilted dramatically backward. It was a Sunday evening in 1974, and Pastor Harold had taken a huge risk and asked me to preach. I was sixteen and had written a masterpiece of a sermon entitled "Don't Kiss Jesus."

My sermon was so bad that I applauded the farmers for not just going home to bed. But what the sermon lacked in content, I made up for with passion. At the end of the message, Pastor Harold got up and put his arm around me and declared, "Listen to me, church. You have just heard a powerful sermon. One of these days, you are going to hear this young man preaching on the radio."

Harold was a man with physical disabilities. He struggled with preaching and leading, and our church never grew above 80 in attendance. Nevertheless, during his ten-year tenure as pastor, ten individuals went into the ministry and have led thousands to Christ. You can google Harold Taves all you want, and you won't find Pastor Harold Taves. But in my mind, there is no doubt that Harold's a hero in heaven. Pastor Harold lived long enough to hear me preach many times on the radio. I wouldn't have been there if not for the way he empowered me.

I call him Reverend Harold "Barnabas" Taves. His gifts were encouragement and empowerment.

One significant handicap to the Church today is that it seems everyone wants to be Paul, and no one is interested in being Barnabas. It's the rare leader, however, who is gifted to the level of a Paul. Every leader, however, can be an empowerer like Barnabas.

Summer is the growing season when the identity of plants becomes apparent. In the spring, you can't easily recognize the difference between the weeds and the wheat. In summer, the plant begins to take on its unique shape and characteristics. Often you can begin to see whether a plant is prioritizing growing for size or growing for fruitfulness. The tallest fruit trees seldom produce the most fruit.

Likewise, leaders in the 25 to 45 age group begin to shape their ministry philosophy and practice it. In their summer, leaders have their first successes, and often you can start to tell whether their priority is the size of their ministry or overall, long-term Kingdom fruitfulness.

In Exponential's research, five levels of churches have been identified:

Level 1: Declining churches
Level 2: Plateaued churches
Level 3: Growing churches
Level 4: Reproducing churches
Level 5: Multiplying churches

Leaders fall into these same five levels in their ministry philosophies and practices. During the summer season, it becomes apparent whether the leader is prioritizing size or impact, addition or multiplication.

When Level 3 leaders meet potential leaders, their first internal question is, "How can this person help me build my thing (church, ministry, non-profit, etc.)?" In other words, "How can they add to what I am doing?"

Level 5 leaders are different. Their first internal question is, "What is this person's calling, and how can I help them accomplish it?" or "How can I empower them into Kingdom impact?

Barnabas lived to empower others into their callings. After Pentecost, he hung out with the apostles in Jerusalem. The one thing we know about that time is that "Joseph" was so empowering to those around him that the apostles gave him the nickname "Barnabas," "son of encouragement." It was so accurate that you don't hear "Joseph" used again. It's "Barnabas" from then on.

The most visible of Barnabas's empowering moments came when Saul was trying to join the disciples of Jesus in Jerusalem. The Christian leaders were understandably skeptical and scared. This was the man who had been hunting them down just a short time ago! There had to be hurt, anger, and resentment toward Saul. But Barnabas saw the Spirit in Saul. Barnabas had probably seen Saul in action in Antioch prior to this. Barnabas took the initiative, introducing Saul to Peter,

James, John, and the other apostles and leaders there. Barnabas vouched for Saul, testifying about his conversion, giftings, and sincerity. He recognized how much impact Saul could have for the Kingdom.

Multipliers are empowerers. They practice these five habits of empowerment to help leaders reach Level 5 (5 for 5):

1. RECOGNIZE them. Recognize leadership potential in others.

Multipliers have their eyes and spirit in "detector mode" continually.

I live at the beach, and I often see folks walking around the sand with their metal detectors. They are looking for coins or for precious metals such as rings. When I look at the area they are working, I sometimes think, "What a waste of time. There's nothing there." Then their detector starts beeping. Soon their little scooper picks up something, and they are shifting through the sand that's buried the treasure. Then they start doing a happy dance. Why? Because they found something of significant value.

Jesus saw something in Peter, James, and John that no one else saw in three ordinary fishermen. Barnabas recognized gold in Paul, in leaders of Antioch, and in John Mark. Paul saw it in Lydia, in Silas, in Timothy. Multipliers are always looking for who they can be empowering. Their leadership detectors are set to "sensitive" mode.

Here are seven traits multipliers are looking for in potential leaders:
1. Spiritual passion: They have zeal for God and his Kingdom work.

2. Servant's heart: They want to help in any way possible because of their passion for the mission. Their faithfulness in small roles opens doors to bigger roles.
3. Influence with people: People are attracted to them. They elevate a room's atmosphere. Their opinion carries weight.
4. Initiative: They don't always wait to be told what to do. They look for what they can do and take action. They anticipate needs and create solutions.
5. Teachability: Good leaders are good followers and easy to coach. They are mission-driven, not ego-driven; therefore, they are not defensive but eager to learn.
6. Emotional intelligence: They are self-aware, self-controlled, empathetic, trustworthy.
7. Mission focused: Helpers love the task, but leaders love the outcomes. They ask the "why" questions and the "How can we do it better?" questions.

2. RELATE to them. Authentic and loving relationships are key to empowering.

I made a serious mistake in my quest to become a multiplier. I wanted to go a mile wide and inch deep. I thought I could just give a church planter some training, run a leadership group, have a few lunches, open a door of ministry for them, and then I would have empowered them. I told them, "I will be here for you. If you have a need, just give me a call. I am your friend."

What happened? Most of them rarely called me. I thought to myself, "Good, that means they are secure in our relationship, and they are doing great." Wrong. There were various reasons they ended up not calling. They were embarrassed by their Sunday attendance numbers, wanting to prove to me and to themselves they could do it without me, not wanting to bother me, etc. As the sending pastor I was in the "power position." The fact that I didn't call them or take them to coffee any longer was disempowering.

Multiplication of leaders and churches always has a vital relational component. Movements flow along relational lines. This is why relational networks are vital to multiplication. Jesus was closer to Peter, James, and John than he was to the rest of the 12. He was closer to the 12 than he was to the 72. He worked through relational proximity. So must we.

What I should have done was slow down and take better care of key planters who could start networks of care with the other planters. Instead, I said "call me," prayed a prayer, and moved on.

Summer is a season to invest in the right relationships—learning to help set realistic expectations of those you invest in, gaining wisdom to create circles of care, not unwisely sacrificing healthy relationships in ego-driven quests for greater ministry success.

3. RISK for them. Risking leadership reputation for them empowers them.

When Barnabas decided to take Saul to the apostles, he was risking his own credibility and reputation. He was aligning himself with a man who had caused severe pain to Christians. There were undoubtedly many who thought, "Saul's scary. He's faking it to get into our circles to arrest us. Saul's not really a Christian. Even if he is, he needs to be marginalized based on what he's done." But Barnabas had seen God's grace in Saul's life. He had watched Saul's character and experienced his gifts being used for Kingdom advance. Barnabas felt led by the Spirit to use his favor and reputation with the apostles and the Christian community in order to see Saul empowered.

It worked. Saul was welcomed into the fellowship. He preached boldly throughout Jerusalem. The Christians there cared for and protected Saul. With the new endorsement of the apostles, Saul would go on to impact the world for Christ.

Saul is not in your church or ministry. But there are plenty of potential leaders who need someone to believe in them enough to take a risk on their behalf. Multipliers learn to take risks in order to empower potential leaders.

After 31 years, Deb and I turned our church over to two young leaders who many considered "high risk." One came out of the largest cult in Mexico; the other had come off the streets of Long Beach. In the last four years, they have gone on to do amazing ministry work. We had a record number of baptisms last year! They have thanked us many times for taking the risk to empower them. Who do *you* need to take a risk on?

4. RESOURCE them. Equip them with the necessary resources.

Many years ago, I tried to build a simple closet in a room at our house. It was so pathetic that my carpenter friend had to come rescue my creative monstrosity. I asked him, "What did I do wrong?" He answered, "Show me your tools, and tell me who trained you." When I did, he shook his head sadly and stated, "You don't have the tools you need, and you have never been trained."

During the summer season, while a leader is growing their ministry, they must also be growing their tool belt. This is the season for going beyond a hammer and a handsaw, graduating to a miter saw and a router. Multipliers seek out those who can equip and train them for the ministry they are building.

Summer is also the time to be handing hammers and saws to emerging leaders. Multipliers are trainers. They empower through imparting the resources their mentees need.
During his summer season, Barnabas (with Saul) spent an entire year teaching believers and training leaders in Antioch (Acts 11:26). There is strong historical and narrative evidence that

Barnabas equipped, trained, and empowered Simeon called
Niger, Lucius of Cyrene, and Manaen, who became leaders in
the church of Antioch (13:1).

5. RELEASE them. Multipliers open doors for their mentees.

The more gifted a mentee is, and the closer we have grown to
them relationally, the harder it is to encourage them to move on
to greater leadership opportunities. Consequently, many pastors
hang on to their mentees far too long. This not only stunts the
growth of the mentee but also shrinks the leadership pipeline in
the Church.

Multipliers actively look for opportunities for their mentees to
minister beyond their current roles. They bless and send their
mentees on to their next ministry assignment.

This, for me, is the most painful part of being a multiplier. In
the church Deb and I led for 31 years, we washed the feet and
sent off over 80 of our best leaders to ministries beyond our
local church. Often my tears were mixed with the water of
foot washing.

What happened because of this "releasing" priority? It communicated that we would empower and send. Emerging leaders
knew they would not be held back. It also created a leadership
vacuum in the church, so that new leaders were always seeing
openings ahead of them.

Barnabas probably wept when he sent his disciple and friend,
John Mark, off to be a part of Paul's ministry team. But
Barnabas was an empowerer, a leader who lived to encourage
the full potential of others and to make the move that would be
best for the Kingdom mission.

Multiplier Insight: Empowering

Leaders who multiply daily integrate being empowered into empowering others. In my Exponential book, *The Empowerment Factor–Increasing Your Personal Multiplication Capacity*, I unpack a tool to help you think of the daily interaction between 1) How empowered you are with the Spirit and 2) How empowering you are to others. Pushing both those factors up is what makes you more like Barnabas and increases your multiplication capacity.

Chapter 8

The Invention That Saved a Million Ships

Multiplier Insight: Giftedness

Multipliers lead from their giftedness to help others discover and use their own giftedness.

The summer season in a multiplier's journey is marked by giftedness emerging through experience—leaders discover what they do best and develop those strengths into their primary contribution.

In the sermon, "The Good Steward," John Wesley emphasizes that every Christian is entrusted with divine gifts—life, time, talents, possessions, and grace—and is called to manage them faithfully for God's glory.[16] Every Christian is gifted, but few Christians (even Christian leaders) have a clear understanding of their giftedness. Consequently, they end up working outside their giftedness and are limited in their ability to help others discover their own giftedness.

---

[16] John Wesley, The Good Steward, in *The Works of John Wesley*, Vol. 7, Sermons 68–86, ed. Albert C. Outler (Nashville: Abingdon Press, 1987), 120.

Focusing Your Light

In the early 1800s, lighthouse lights were dim, unpredictable flames. Ships continued to crash because the light didn't project far enough to guide them. Then Augustin Fresnel developed a remarkable, multi-layered glass lens that focused the flame into a powerful beam—bright enough to reach the horizon. His creation was sometimes called "the invention that saved a million ships."

What changed the world wasn't a stronger flame—it was a clearer lens. Fresnel's creation worked on two primary principles: refraction (focusing the light from broad to narrow) and reflection (capturing light that was otherwise wasted). When these two principles worked together, the light could be cast for miles to warn ships of the danger ahead.

Refraction speaks to the focusing of a leader's time and energy. Clarity of gifting and calling is essential to effectiveness. The clearer a leader is, the further they can send their light and the more "ships" that can be saved.

Leaders are living with diffused light. They equate busyness with proving their ministry value. They want to do too much in too many places to please too many people.

After his first retirement, Michael Jordan pursued professional baseball—his father's dream for him. Despite his legendary athleticism, he hit only .202 in the minor leagues and struggled in nearly every metric. What felt like a "good idea" simply wasn't his gift.

When he returned to basketball, he immediately reclaimed dominance, winning three more NBA championships and cementing himself as one of the greatest players of all time.

Even Jordan couldn't manufacture giftedness. He had to focus on his area of maximum impact.

Capturing Your Energy

Reflection in Fresnel's model speaks to capturing wasted time and energy. It is recognizing the time and energy being spent outside one's primary calling and gifting, then reclaiming that for the pursuits most essential to the mission. It's what my nuclear engineer friend calls, "eliminating sideways energy."

Leaders have plenty of time to do all God is calling them to do, but not enough time to do all that people want them to do. Leaders must grow their no.

My wife is fond of saying, "*No* is a complete sentence." She also admonishes me, "Larry, just remember every *yes* is a *no* to something else." It goes with her "closet principle." She won't buy a new piece of clothing unless she gives away something from her closet. That's why she can find things in her closet, and I can't.

Reflection is the process of throwing out the clutter of our lives and using that space for what matters most, what fits our giftedness best. Greg McKeown, in his insightful book *Essentialism: The Disciplined Pursuit of Less* writes, "It's about making the wisest possible investment of your time and energy in order to operate at your highest point of contribution."[17]

---

[17] Greg McKeown, *Essentialism: The Disciplined Pursuit of Less* (New York: Crown Business, 2014), 6.

Refusing Gift Envy

Much of the lack of focus is due to pastors' propensity to waste energy trying to be more like some uniquely gifted pastor in some very different context than their own. Gift envy is an energy drain. God warns us about the sin of comparison and beckons us to the pleasure of "gift contentment." The apostle Paul writes, "Let each one test his own work, and then his reason to boast will be in himself alone and not in his neighbor" (Galatians 6:4).

Barnabas never tried to be Paul. Paul was a profound theologian and forceful organizational leader. Barnabas was an inspirational leader who constantly encouraged, affirmed, and restored.

Barnabas softened edges, strengthened people, built unity, and nurtured emerging leaders. Paul advanced mission, sharpened doctrine, confronted error, and expanded the church. They each operated in their unique giftedness. Together they formed a powerful team, a leadership ecosystem.

Summer is weed-pulling time. In spring the seeds are planted. In summer they grow, but so do the weeds. In his parable of the soils, Jesus talked about the thistles and weeds that choke out the plant as it tries to grow. Weeds are anything that robs the plant of the water, nutrients, space, or sun it needs in order to thrive.

In the summer season, the multiplier gets clear about what is wheat and what is weeds, about what is their primary gifting and what is not. They become vigilant about weed-pulling. If they don't, their ministry will not reach its full potential.

Most folks don't know that C. S. Lewis desired to be a poet. His first published works—*Spirits in Bondage* (1919) and "Dymer" (1926)—were poetry. His poetry, however, received little recognition, and Lewis himself later admitted that he simply did not possess the poetic genius he admired in others. Lewis could have tried harder, instead he refocused. At age 34, in his summer season, Lewis stopped writing poetry and wrote his first book. In doing so, he discovered the lane he was born to run in: imaginative fiction, Christian apologetics, and theological writing. Lewis would have missed his maximum impact if he hadn't pulled the weeds. Do you have some weeds that need pulling?

A Clearer Understanding of Giftedness

According to Robert Clinton, "Giftedness is a combination of natural abilities, acquired skills, and spiritual gifts."[18] Our giftedness is an interplay between these three.

Natural abilities are those capacities, skills, talents, or aptitudes that are innate in a person and allow them to accomplish things. (Examples: analytical bent, intuition, and relational aptitude)

Acquired skills are those capacities, skills, talents, or aptitudes that have been learned by a person in order to allow them to accomplish something. (Examples: writing, motivational skills, playing piano, and any skills learned over time)

Spiritual gifts are a God-given, unique, supernatural capacity imparted for the purpose of releasing Holy Spirit-empowered acts, both within the church and in the world. (Examples: discerning spirits, healings, word of knowledge, teaching, evangelism, apostleship)

---

[18] Clinton, J. Robert. *Understanding Our Giftedness Set* (Spiritual-Gifting Worksheet). Retrieved from https://storage2.snappages.site/G5FQ3S/assets/files/Spiritual-Gifting-Worksheet-CLINTON.pdf

How does a leader discover their giftedness?

1. Giftedness emerges through ministry involvement.
Giftedness is discovered through dirty hands. Gifts are not
discovered or developed in isolation but in active engagement
in spiritual work. Ministry involvement brings specific giftedness
to the surface. Spiritual gift inventories are helpful tools to help
us understand ourselves, but they follow spiritual work. They
look back on the ministry work we have done and help us know
ourselves better.

Barnabas spent approximately 10 years in Jerusalem actively
serving in ministry before he was chosen to go to Antioch. His
gifts emerged during this ministry work.

**2. Giftedness is identified through patterns
of effectiveness.**
God uses us beyond our own abilities on many occasions and
in many different ways. This is his anointing and grace. Our
primary giftedness, however, includes anointing but moves
beyond it to embedded effectiveness. It is a recurring pattern
of discernible impact whenever we operate in a particular area
of ministry. It seems to come naturally to you and consistently
works when you do it.

After overcoming a stuttering problem, I attempted public
speaking in my local 4-H club at the ripe age of 11. I gave
a riveting talk on raising rabbits. To my surprise, I won first
place. Four years later, I was winning debate contests. Four
years after that, I was in a college preaching class and was voted
most powerful preacher. I began to see a pattern of giftedness.
Consequently, I dedicated my life to public speaking for Jesus.
Fifty years of preaching have followed that. What patterns are
you seeing in your life?

3. Giftedness produces an inner confirmation of joy and satisfaction.
When you are operating in your giftedness there is a sense of God's smile on you, a deep fulfillment, a sense of God's presence, an inner energy, and a flow to your work.

My wife, Dr. Deb is a professional counselor, mentor, and pastor. One of the most potent questions she asks believers to wrestle with is, "Does this make your heart sing?" Operating in your giftedness is what stirs a song in your spirit. For example, whenever my wife has a Zoom call with her mentees, her face lights up, her energy increases, and she talks faster. She is gifted in this area, and it shows in her countenance.

4. Giftedness is affirmed by the feedback of others.
"Community discernment" describes believers who know us speaking into what they are seeing in us. Repeated affirmations inform our understanding of our giftedness. The apostles were so affirming of Joseph they gave him the nickname "Barnabas," "son of encouragement."

Dave Ferguson in his book *Hero Maker* popularized the four-letter acronym ICNU, encouraging believers to speak into the lives of others using the words "I see in you."

Barnabas comes across in Scripture as perhaps the most impactful leader who used ICNU to encourage people into their giftedness (Acts 11:25-26). Multipliers listen to what others see in them. Multipliers speak affirmation, encouragement, and destiny into the lives of others.

5. Giftedness is discerned by open doors in front of you.
When discerning giftedness, one needs to look for doors God is opening, situations that are arising, connections that are

happening with people of influence, invitations that seem divinely orchestrated, random connections and opportunities.

God's providence helps reveal gifting. God often opens doors in alignment with your primary giftedness.

Multipliers are always looking for doors they can open for other believers. When multipliers see gifts in their disciples, they start looking for opportunities for those gifts to be used.

6. Giftedness is revealed through obedience.

When you obey what you *know* to do for Jesus, you begin to see more clearly what you were *wired* to do for Jesus. A critical mass of experiences in which you have simply obeyed what Jesus was telling you to do is essential in gaining clarity about your primary giftedness.

Paul writes in 2 Timothy 4:5, "Do the work of an evangelist." Most scholars note that Timothy's primary giftings were shepherding and teaching. He may not have been naturally bold, outgoing, or gifted in evangelism. But Paul is exhorting him, "Even if evangelism is not your dominant gift, it is still your essential work." Through obedience to *commanded* work, Timothy's *chosen* work became more clear.

7. Giftedness is a gift mix—a dominant gift supported by other supporting gifts.

In studying the lives of biblical and church history leaders, you generally see a predominant gift accompanied by other comple- mentary gifts. This gift mix is a combination that you repeatedly express with effectiveness.

Barnabas had the dominant gift of encouragement (Acts 11:23). He also had leading, teaching, giving, and discerning gifts. Encouragement was the gravitational center of his ministry identity. He is the prototype of a multiplier: one who believes in others, draws out their gifts, and creates environments where leaders can grow and use their gifts. He helped launch people into their destiny.

How Multipliers Encourage and Invest in the Giftedness of Others

Multipliers believe that every believer has a Spirit-given contribution (1 Corinthians 12:4-7; Ephesians 4:7-13), and they make it their mission to help people discover, develop, and deploy that contribution.

10 Ways Multipliers Do This:

1. Multipliers see giftedness in others before others see it in themselves.
2. Multipliers name giftedness out loud.
3. Multipliers create environments for safe experimentation with giftedness.
4. Multipliers give permission and blessing.
5. Multipliers provide training and tools to develop giftedness.
6. Multipliers offer appropriate challenges. (A challenge without encouragement crushes. Encouragement without challenge stagnates. Multipliers integrate both.)
7. Multipliers model a life worth imitating. (Giftedness grows in imitation-rich environments; Philippians 3:17; 1 Corinthians 11:1. Multipliers live transparently in community. People learn giftedness by watching giftedness.)
8. Multipliers invest relationally.
9. Multipliers delegate meaningful responsibility. (Not busywork—real work, like Jesus sending the disciples out two by two in Mark 6 and Luke 10. Multipliers believe people grow by doing, not just by watching and listening.)
10. Multipliers help leaders find the intersection between their primary gifting and their primary contribution.

Multiplier Insight: Giftedness

Leaders who multiply understand that the Spirit is intent on multiplying both the quantity and quality of spiritual gifts active in his church. This makes their commitment to discovering, developing, and deploying our gifts—and equipping others to do likewise—essential.

Chapter 9

Augustine and the Young Gun

Multiplier Insight:
Humility

Multipliers pursue Kingdom fruitfulness not personal prestige.

One of the greatest ministry leadership letters ever written was penned 1600 years ago by Augustine. In it he wrote these now famous words: "If you ask me what the essential thing in religion and discipline is, I will answer: first, humility; second, humility; and third, humility."[19]

Dioscorus was a "young gun," a gifted emerging leader just entering his summer season of life. He was a young Roman nobleman living in Carthage around A.D. 410. Dioscorus possessed intellect, social status, rhetorical training, and a spiritual zeal.

Augustine was 55 years old and already one of the great pastors and theologians of the church. But Augustine was also a multiplier. He saw in Dioscorus a young man whose gifts could be shaped for significant Kingdom impact. So, Augustine began

---

[19] Augustine, Letter 118.22, in *Nicene and Post-Nicene Fathers, First Series, vol. 1*, ed. Philip Schaff (Peabody, MA: Hendrickson, 1994), 465.

a mentoring relationship that resulted in Letter 118, the only surviving letter of their friendship.

In this letter Augustine does not focus on talent, ambition, skills, or public ministry. Instead, he tells Dioscorus that the first, second, and third essential of the Christian life is humility. Augustine understood that humility causes dependency upon God, and this is the life God can bless and empower. He knew giftedness without humility eventually spoils the fruit of ministry and the minister themselves.

Augustine knew what John Stott would write 15 centuries later: "At every stage of our Christian development, and in every sphere of our Christian discipleship, pride is the greatest enemy and humility our greatest friend."[20]

Summer Realities

The summer season of life and ministry (roughly 25 to 45 in age) is a time of growing. In summer, fruit becomes visible—tomatoes appear, wheat waves in the wind, grapes cluster on the vine. Likewise, leaders begin to see ministry impacting, giftedness manifesting, influence growing, doors opening, notoriety blooming. This is the danger zone. Summer fruit can feed pride unless humility is deeply rooted.

Summer also brings heat, and heat exposes the health of the plant. It reveals what is unseen, the depth of the roots. Summer's heat exposes the humility or pride hidden beneath ministry activity.

---

[20] John R. W. Stott, *The Cross of Christ* (Downers Grove, IL: InterVarsity Press, 1986), 284.

Summer discloses whether a tree is going to prioritize growing bigger or growing fruit. When Jesus saw the fig tree, he was not impressed with its size or all its leaves, but he was keenly interested in whether it had fruit. Size and leaves on a tree are great to look at, but fruit carries the seed that can be planted and multiplied.

Humility prioritizes fruit over size. Or in church multiplication language, "Humility prioritizes Kingdom over castle." The success of summer's growth will determine whether a leader uses it to build their castle or invests it in Kingdom multiplication.

My Summer Season

In my summer season, our church became the fastest-growing church in our denomination. My dream was to become a megachurch after relocating from a building with only 39 parking spaces. God interrupted that dream with a revelation that sent us on a different trajectory.

Through Ezekiel 47 he showed me that we had built a "lake" church, where people flowed in to build my ministry and we did everything we could to keep them so the lake would grow bigger. His direction to us was to radically shift the culture to be a "river" church, where people would flow in but then flow back out to start life-giving churches in other locations. Rather than being a church of addition, we would become a multiplication church, starting new churches in dead places. Our castle might not grow any bigger, but the Kingdom would.

My ego did not like this new vision. It threatened my self-image, which was rooted in my visible success. I wanted my summer season to grow a bigger tree, without thinking about planting new trees. Thankfully, the Spirit worked through my wife to ask me the questions that uncovered the pride that was resisting the call of the Spirit. I repented and started seeking the humility that I knew I needed so much more of.

The Humility of Barnabas

Barnabas is the epitome of the humility necessary to drive multiplication. His humility is not merely a personality trait—it is a Kingdom posture that fuels multiplication. Nearly every appearance he makes in Acts reveals a leader willing to take the lower place so others can flourish.

Consider these three examples from the summer season (Acts 9:1–13:1) of Barnabas's ministry:

When the early church feared Saul, Barnabas stood with him, vouched for him, and brought him to the apostles (Acts 9:27). This is humility. Proud leaders protect their own status. Humble leaders risk their reputation to elevate someone with potential. Barnabas didn't ask, "How will this affect me?" But "How will this help Saul and the mission?"

Barnabas humbly submitted to the authority of the leaders of the church in Jerusalem. He was sent to Antioch to check out the legitimacy of the gospel movement reported there. Barnabas was assigned a role, sent on a mission, and commissioned by leadership (Acts 11:22). He went not on his own authority but on the authority of apostles. This submission to leadership surfaces again in Acts 13 and Acts 15.

"Who sent you?" is a key question I ask when new church planters arrive in Long Beach. In church planting today, too many planters are sending themselves. They have chosen to forego spiritual accountability in their lives. Submission to godly authority is a command in Scripture, but it requires a humility that is scarce in leaders today.

Barnabas humbly recruited leaders more gifted than himself (Acts 11:25-26). The church in Antioch was burgeoning with growth. Barnabas was the "lead pastor" in one of the most significant spiritual movements in the first century. He could have been the pope of Antioch. Instead, Barnabas traveled for 400 miles—20 days one way—to recruit Saul to help co-lead the work. He elevated a leader who was younger, more educated, more gifted in teaching and leadership.

Proud leaders fear being overshadowed. They are skeptical of gifted leaders, often looking for reasons to discount them and keep them in lower positions. Humble multipliers recruit and empower people who will surpass them.

Barnabas humbly shared leadership and even relinquished the first chair for the sake of the mission. In Antioch, Barnabas is always listed first—until he and Saul (Paul) step into apostolic ministry. By Acts 13:43, the order reverses: "Paul and Barnabas." Barnabas doesn't resist the shift. He doesn't demand recognition or cling to position. His humility helped grow Paul into a leader who could surpass him in position and impact.

For Barnabas it wasn't about himself; it was about the mission. Renowned business author Jim Collins writes about Level 5 leaders saying, "They possess 'a compelling modesty' and 'channel their ambition into the cause, not themselves.'"[21]

---

[21] Jim Collins, *Good to Great: Why Some Companies Make the Leap … and Others Don't* (New York: HarperBusiness, 2001), 21.

Humility and Multipliers

The summer season of life determines whether true humility or self-advancement will be the essence of your ministry. Successes can inflate your ego, become your identity, and replace dependency upon the Spirit. Setbacks can undermine your identity, threaten your call, reduce your faith, and trap you in comparison. True humility is freeing, empowering, and multiplicative.

7 Markers of Humility That Empower Multipliers

1. Security in identity not ministry

Having done ministry for 50 years, I have struggled with my value being in what my current ministry success looks like compared to that of other ministers. But I want to be so secure in who I am in Christ that I can live and minister with boldness and freedom.

One of my battle weapons is the Lord's Prayer. When I pray it daily, I pause at each phrase and expand it into my own words. When I pray, "Our Father," I focus on who he is and who I am in him. I pray, "Lord, my highest title and the greatest truth about me is that I am your beloved son who serves." The more I live in the fullness of this truth, the freer I am.

One of my biblical heroes is John the Baptist. Jesus identified him as the greatest who has ever lived (Matthew 11:11). Yet, John's ministry was consumed with pointing away from himself to Jesus. Statements like "I am just a voice" and "I am not worthy to untie his sandals" display his humility.

John's disciples grew insecure when Jesus and *his* disciples were baptizing more people than them, but John was unfazed and stated, "He must become greater; I must become less"

(John 3:30). His identity was not in his ministry. He knew who he was in God, what his calling was, and the power of focusing all attention on Jesus instead of himself. This gave him a ministry boldness that could call out the sin of kings (Matthew 14:4) and the security to "send" his disciples out to new ministry (John 1:35-37).

Insecure leaders will invest in those who don't threaten their status, position, or self-image. Multipliers, however, are so secure in their identity and self-worth in Christ that they are eager to empower those who will outshine them.

Questions:
1. Do I derive more joy from being used by God or being loved by God—and what does that reveal about where my identity is rooted?
2. If all my ministry roles were stripped away tomorrow, would I still feel secure in who I am in Christ?

2. Deep dependency

Humility is living keenly aware of our absolute dependency upon God. We often quote Jesus saying, "Apart from me you can do nothing," but then we work like it all depends on us.

The primary barometer of dependency is how saturated with prayer the air of your ministry is. Pastors tend to overwork and under-pray. They work too much at the things that produce too little fruit. Prayer reveals what God wants you to do, then it gives you the power to do it. Prayer opens doors your efforts could never open and supplies resources you could never acquire.

Multipliers embrace their inability to produce spiritual fruit on their own. A branch doesn't strain to grow fruit; instead it abides more deeply in the vine. If a leader doesn't learn this in their summer years, it will poison the rest of their ministry unless they repent of self-reliance.

Questions:
1. Where in my current leadership am I functioning more out of skill and experience than out of prayerful dependence?
2. When was the last time I chose a path that required God's power—not just my competence—to succeed?

3. Coachability

The humble are easy to coach. They are eager to learn. They aren't defensive. Their self-image is not threatened by correction. It doesn't make you uptight when you have to tell them something hard. This distinction is captured in Proverbs 9:8-9 (NIV): "Do not rebuke mockers or they will hate you; rebuke the wise and they will love you. Instruct the wise and they will be wiser still."

Over time, I've learned there are growlers, and there are growers. Growlers resist feedback—they complain, grumble, make excuses, dismiss counsel, or rationalize away correction. Growers respond differently. They embrace instruction, learn from correction, express gratitude, hold themselves accountable, and lean in when coaching and teaching are offered.

Some people think the better you get, the harder you are to coach. But in the NFL, coaches will tell you the opposite. Peyton Manning—one of the greatest quarterbacks of all time—was also one of the easiest to coach. Even as a superstar, he invited correction, asked questions, and made adjustments immediately. He would often request of his coaches, "Coach me hard." He didn't resist coaching because he was great; he was great because he stayed coachable.

The more coachable you are in summer, the more fruitful you will be in autumn and winter.

Questions:
1. How do I typically respond when someone corrects me—emotionally, verbally, internally—and what does that say about my humility?
2. Who has permission to challenge me, and when was the last time I allowed someone to sharpen or redirect me?

4. People-building (over platform-building)

Humility is the key to whether you will prioritize building your own brand or helping others become all they can be. Paul put it clearly, "Knowledge puffs up while love builds up" (1 Corinthians 8:1, NIV). There are many "puffed up" leaders who want to use people to build their own platform. But loving leaders want to serve people, to help them build a platform they can stand on.

Barnabas was a "people builder." He was never pushing his own name or declaring his own position. Instead, he built up the Antioch Christians, Saul, the poor, John Mark, and others.

Questions:
1. Am I investing more time in developing people than in developing my brand, network, platform excellence, or visibility?
2. Would I be content if the leaders I develop receive more recognition than I ever do?

5. Sacrificial releasing

Humility not only builds others more than self, but it releases them into God's best for their lives. Many leaders build people in order to build their own ministry. But when you build leaders with an open hand, you freely send them into what God has next for them.

Our gifted youth pastor, J.R., helped Deb and me plant our first church plant. It was thriving. About a year into the plant, J.R. came to me and shared that God was telling him to go to the east coast to plant. He asked for my opinion, and I told him I thought he had misheard the Lord. I had big plans for him! I needed him to help build my thing, not go do his own thing. But then the Spirit spoke to me clearly, "Do you want the best for yourself or for J.R. and my Kingdom?" J.R. went to the east coast and planted a vibrant church. I was 42, and that lesson opened the door for 25 years of raising up and releasing.

Questions:
1. Do I hesitate to empower others because I fear being replaced, overlooked, or forgotten? What does that reveal?
2. Do I slow down the "sending" of a leader or church planter for fear of how it may impact what I am building?

6. Joyful collaboration

Humble people find collaboration easy to do. Not so with the proud. God promised, "Two are better than one, because they have a good return for their toil" (Ecclesiastes 4:9). Jesus sent them out in pairs. Barnabas was always working with partners.

The popular quote may be overused, (probably because it is so true), but "If you want to go fast, go alone; if you want to go far, go together." Collaboration is always slower and better. If you don't learn this in your summer season, your autumn will be less fruitful and your winter will be more lonely.

Questions:
1. Do I genuinely enjoy sharing leadership, or do I subtly pull back when others' gifts overshadow mine?

2. In my team contexts, do people feel valued and
    empowered—or managed and constrained?

7. Rests in God's sovereignty

Humility is only healthy when it is rooted in God's great
personal love for us. Because of his love and his power, we can
humble ourselves to rest in his plans for us. We can work from
a position of trust, knowing that we are not the ones who are
responsible for the results—only for our obedience and faith.

Questions:
1. Where am I striving, grasping, or forcing outcomes rather
    than trusting God's timing and direction?
2. Do I experience peace when God elevates others instead of
    me—or does it expose areas of discontent or mistrust?

Multiplier Insight: Humility

Leaders who multiply are seeking to live into the power of
humility and wholehearted trust in God's sovereignty as
expressed in John Wesley's Covenant Prayer. Every true multiplier must practice this prayer. I suggest you stop right now and
slowly read it through a few times until you can pray it from
your heart:

I am no longer my own, but Thine.
Put me to what Thou wilt, rank me with whom Thou wilt.
Put me to doing, put me to suffering.
Let me be employed for Thee or laid aside for Thee,
exalted for Thee or brought low for Thee.
Let me be full, let me be empty.
Let me have all things, let me have nothing.
I freely and heartily yield all things
to Thy pleasure and disposal.
And now, O glorious and blessed God,

Father, Son, and Holy Spirit,
Thou art mine, and I am Thine. So be it.
And the covenant which I have made on earth,
let it be ratified in heaven.
Amen.

Chapter 10

What VISA and Multiplication Have in Common

Multiplier Insight: Chaordic

Multipliers embrace the chaordic nature of Spirit-led ministry.

Roughly 50% of you reading this have a VISA credit card. You can thank Dee Hock. Mr. Hock was the founder and long-time CEO of VISA International and the creator of the word *chaordic*. Mr. Hock was reflecting on the principles that had led to the unexpected global success of VISA and coined the word *chaordic* to summarize it.

Chaordic blends the characteristics of chaos and order in generative, life-giving ways. Hock argued that the most resilient, adaptive, and scalable organizations operate in the dynamic tension between chaos and order. When I read the book of Acts and think of multiplication, I see the beauty and power of "chaordic."

I love jazz music. Jazz is an excellent metaphor for chaordic because it embodies the creative tension between order and freedom. Jazz musicians do not play at random; they agree on a shared structure—key, tempo, rhythm, and chord progression—that gives order to the music. Yet within those boundaries, they improvise in real time, responding to one another, the moment, and the movement of the piece itself. The music is neither rigidly scripted nor chaotically uncontrolled. It is ordered enough to be recognizable and free enough to be alive.

Chaordic in Acts

When we study the book of Acts, we find a "Spirit-led" and "apostolic-taught" church (Acts 2). The first-century church lived in the creative tension between order and freedom, structure and spontaneity, shared doctrine and local expression. It was neither chaotic nor rigidly centralized, but spiritually alive.

Long before *chaordic* was in a dictionary, the church evidenced its characteristics: clear and compelling mission, simple governing principles, distributed authority, and interdependence. Over time, however, the church declined into more of an institution than an organic movement. It moved away from "chaordic" into "control" with a rigid authoritarian structure. This squeezed the life of the Spirit out of the church as a movement.

But in the first century, leaders like Barnabas epitomized the chaordic leaders needed to instigate the rapid movement of the church. Barnabas was the Spirit-led *and* apostolic-taught leader who could embrace the messiness of movements and the need for simple, empowering structure.

The chaordic leader must passionately pursue this dynamic middle. Chaordic leadership requires a fundamental shift in mindset—it requires leaders who are no longer architects designing every component of the system, nor commanders issuing detailed instructions. Instead, they become gardeners cultivating conditions in which healthy growth can occur. They are culture creators.

Chaordic leadership includes:
1. Clarifying and guarding the organization's purpose/mission
2. Articulating and modeling core values
3. Nurturing key relationships for personal and missional purposes
4. Designing simple, empowering structures rather than controlling mechanisms
5. Trusting people with real authority and frontline decision-making
6. Allowing experimentation, failure, and learning

Barnabas the Chaordic Leader

As you study the life and leadership of Barnabas, you find each of these six characteristics clearly demonstrated.

When Barnabas advocates for Saul in Jerusalem (Acts 9:26-27), he takes a risk that institutional leaders were unwilling to take. Barnabas does not demand guarantees or impose lengthy probation. He listens, discerns, and then lends his credibility to Saul. In doing so, he opens space for one of the most significant leadership trajectories in church history. Chaordic leaders create trust bridges made of relationship rather than regulation. Barnabas's influence flowed through credibility and character, not command and control.

The church in Antioch was not a centrally planned initiative (Acts 11:19-21). Believers scattered by persecution began preaching to Gentiles, and the Spirit moved powerfully. When Jerusalem leaders heard about it, they sent Barnabas to discern whether God was at work. They trusted Barnabas to have a balanced view of what was happening.

When Barnabas arrived, he "saw the grace of God" and rejoiced (Acts 11:23). This is a quintessential chaordic moment. Movements are messy. He probably saw a bit of organic chaos but also the order of essential doctrines. Instead of imposing a Jerusalem model on Antioch, Barnabas strengthened what was already emerging. He encouraged faithfulness to the Lord while allowing the form to remain locally adapted.

Chaordic leaders rely on a small set of guiding principles rather than exhaustive policies. Barnabas's life reveals consistent patterns: generosity, encouragement, inclusion, faith in God's work in people, Holy Spirit reliance, and loyalty to the mission. These principles guided his decisions across vastly different contexts—Jerusalem, Antioch, Cyprus, and beyond. Because his leadership was principle-driven, not procedure-bound, Barnabas could respond wisely in unpredictable situations.

The Chaordic Summer

Summer is when growth accelerates beyond the farmer's direct control. Plants stretch toward the sun. Roots expand underground unseen. Weather patterns assert themselves. This is inherently chaordic.

The farmer cannot dictate how fast the plant grows, only whether conditions support healthy growth. Attempting to control summer growth—by over-pruning, over-watering, or constant disturbance—often does more harm than good. Letting plants grow on their own without any rhythms of caretaking also damages the harvest.

The summer season of leadership is typically marked by rapid growth, expanding responsibility, high energy, and increasing influence. Leaders in this stage are often discovering what they can do—and just as importantly, how they tend to do it. It is a season of building, experimenting, stretching capacity, and learning through action rather than theory. For this reason, it is also the season where chaordic leadership emerges most naturally.

The summer season is where leaders:
- Learn to lead through influence or control
- Decide whether to centralize authority in themselves or to distribute authority
- Choose whether to trust complex strategies or the guidance of the Spirit's simple strategies
- Decide whether to take risks that might create messes or to grow overprotective
- Choose whether multiplication or addition will be the priority

Those who learn the beauty of chaordic leadership in this season carry its fruit into autumn and legacy. Those who suppress it usually struggle later to release control.

Barnabas shows us that leaders who embrace chaordic instincts early—anchored in truth and mission, guided by the Spirit, and generous with authority—become the quiet architects of multiplication.

The End of My CEOism

Toward the end of my summer season (age 41 for me), the church Deb and I were leading was called to start planting churches. I was not a chaordic leader. I was a CEO type of pastor who was following a detailed strategy to keep getting bigger. I told the Lord, "I don't know the first thing about how to plant a church. I am going to make a mess of this. What should I do?" He seemed to respond, "Pray and obey." I told the Lord, "That's no strategic plan!"

God was saying, "Seek my Spirit through prayer, and I will start guiding you step by step—if you obey." So we told the church about our Ezekiel 47 river vision of people flowing into our church for a time then flowing back out to start new churches. Then we called for 40 days of fasting and prayer. The Lord counseled me that he was going to do a work I could influence but not control. If I tried to carefully manage it, it would die. But if I empowered it, and would tolerate the messiness of it, it would multiply.

Now 26 years later, with 35 church plants in the U.S. and another 100+ more in three different countries, I understand some of what I needed to unlearn and learn. Strategic plans are helpful but inadequate for multiplication. I have to 1) seek the Spirit and respond to his direction, 2) embrace the supernatural opportunities he presents but I didn't plan, 3) decentralize authority by raising up and releasing other pastors, and 4) be willing to risk and fail in the world's eyes.

When I began to practice this approach, a bit of chaos started happening. I wasn't trying to control how many or who were leaving our church to start a new one. I was no longer in charge of where we planted next. I didn't worry about which tithers were going. I was no longer protecting our "brand." But there was enough order in our preparation of church planters to keep things from descending into chaos.

To pursue the chaordic leadership path of the Holy Spirit:

1. Re-anchor leadership identity in purpose not position.

Leaders are often rewarded early in their summer season for competence, decisiveness, and output. Chaordic leadership begins when leaders re-anchor their identity in WHY they lead rather than HOW MUCH they manage. When identity is secured in WHO they are in Christ, and WHY they are ministering, then they can be Kingdom-focused instead of career-focused. Practically, this means clarifying the mission you will not compromise, the values that will guide decisions, and the outcomes you must trust God to produce.

Barnabas modeled this by rejoicing when he "saw the grace of God" already at work (Acts 11:23), even when it unfolded outside his direct influence. He didn't come to Antioch to further his ministry, to stroke his ego, to assume a position, or to control. He came to extend the Kingdom by asking how his gifts and leadership could serve.

2. Practice giving away real authority early.

Chaordic leadership cannot be learned by theory alone—it must be practiced through release. Typical summer-season leaders often wait too long to empower others, assuming readiness must be proven before trust is granted. Chaordic leaders reverse the order: trust becomes the pathway to readiness.

Jesus modeled this with the 72 disciples he sent out who were still very much in training. Barnabas modeled this when he recruited Saul into leadership before his reputation was fully rehabilitated.

3. Learn to lead with simple principles instead of detailed rules.

Summer leaders often overbuild systems because clarity feels safer than ambiguity. Chaordic leadership teaches leaders to replace complex rulebooks with simple, non-negotiable principles.

Invariably in older organizations you find voluminous pages of policies. These have been written to guard the organization from mistakes made in the past. But instead of guarding the organization, they suffocate it. Organizations produce manuals. Movements reduce manuals. This is what the Jerusalem Council did. The Holy Spirit spoke, and what happened? Clarity and simplification (Acts 15:28-29).

4. Deepen trust in the Holy Spirit to work beyond you. At its core, chaordic leadership is spiritual trust. It assumes that the Holy Spirit is already at work in people, places, and processes the leader does not directly control. When the work belongs to the Lord, the Spirit will work to propel it, to safeguard it, to correct it, to do the unexpected, to move it in ways you may never hear about.

Recently I was at a conference and a nicely dressed woman who looked vaguely familiar came up to me. She asked, "Pastor Larry, do you remember me? A few years ago I was in your church for a short time before we moved to Texas. You taught about being a river church that sends out people to plant churches. The Holy Spirit spoke to me and asked me to plant a church in the city we moved to. Now 80 people attend, and we have sent out church planters to start new churches."

The Holy Spirit had birthed daughter and granddaughter churches that I didn't know about and that didn't know me. I celebrated something the Spirit did outside my control, but through our church that was willing to become chaordic.

5. Expect messiness as the price of multiplication.

One of the hardest lessons for summer leaders to learn is that multiplication is always messier than management. Chaordic leadership chooses scalable mess over fragile neatness.

The chaordic creates enough space and freedom for more leaders to arise more quickly, even spontaneously. New Testament churches were birthed quickly as the movement spread. The result? The Gospel was preached, the Kingdom expanded, and messes were made. Of the 27 books in the New Testament, at least 21 were written primarily or substantially to address real problems, tensions, sins, or challenges in churches or among believers.

When we were raising our daughter, at first we would spoon-feed her and wipe her mouth after every bite. She would reach for the spoon, and we wouldn't let her have it because if she got hold of it, a mess would follow. But soon we realized that if we kept control of feeding her, we might not have a mess, but we would also have a daughter who never fed herself. The mess was a part of her development and would bring freedom to us and to her. Our leadership requires letting purposeful messes develop.

Multiplier Insight: Chaordic

Leaders who multiply pray to capture the balance represented in "chaordic" leadership. How leaders develop during the summer season determines whether they end up just adding or moving into multiplication, whether they go on to building movements or only managing institutions. Those who embrace chaordic leadership in summer carry its fruit into autumn and legacy—these are leaders who know how to ignite movement, not just lead systems.

AUTUMN

"It's the first day of autumn!
A time of hot chocolatey mornings,
and toasty marshmallow evenings, and, best of all,
leaping into leaves!"

— Winnie the Pooh

It has been said that autumn is nature's proof that change can be beautiful. This season is called fall in the United States because during this season leaves fall from the trees. Temperatures begin to cool, and days become shorter as the season progresses. Days are shorter as night becomes longer. This change is felt not only in the weather but also in the natural world, as plants and animals prepare for the coming winter. The most striking feature of autumn is the astounding color change of the leaves as they prepare to release and fall to the ground. In many ways, autumn parallels spring. Life seems to start all over again when the crisp autumn air settles in.

During the autumn development season (ages 49 to 64) leaders who multiply experience the power of prime. We live in a world that is addicted to youth. It is great news for the Christian leader that our prime begins in our 50s. During autumn God brings a convergence of three leadership components: 1) character—we have proven faithful and passed our integrity tests to become wise, gentle, leaders who can be trusted; 2) gifts—we have proven faithful to develop our spiritual gifts so that people experience God's power when we minister; and 3) role—we have proven faithful in seeking God for his strategic wisdom as we have chosen, and often crafted, a role that aligns with our gifts and destiny. During this season leaders who multiply will often maximize their gifts and deliver ministry that will become their ultimate contribution. As new as the autumn season can feel, we know that the cold winter will one day arrive. The beauty of autumn is its reminder that even though beautiful things have to end, the raw beauty of winter is full of God's grace.

The data for Barnabas's autumn season is found in Acts 13:1–14:28. Barnabas, the son of encouragement, full of the Holy Spirit, was chosen to be the advanced scout of the Antioch church plant because of his tested character. At Antioch, Barnabas developed his gifts of apostleship, leadership, exhortation, and giving. He not only identified his gifts but did the hard work of turning his 10 into 100. Barnabas faithfully obeyed and followed the Holy Spirit into his ideal role of church planting mentor. Barnabas's autumn season ended with the faithful (and painful) apostolic work of planting the church at Galatia.

I (John) am in the first third of my autumn season. Autumn for me arrived unexpectedly with a tiny coronavirus-19 that shut down the world. Over the last five years, God has brought so much life through a "later-in-life faith challenge." My world was turned upside down at age 50 when God answered my wife's desperate prayers by sending fire from heaven twice in a 10-day period. We have since followed Jesus into planting a new church in Compton. I have been commissioned by the Clinton family to write a new version of Dr. Clinton's classic The Making of a Leader. This season has been full of unmerited graces, divine affirmation, and destiny fulfillment. I have no certainty how this autumn season will end. But I thank God every day for my life in God, my family, and an ideal role to deliver ministry that aligns with my gifts.

In the next five chapters, we unpack the third major development stage of Barnabas's life. Larry and I pray the Holy Spirit will encourage you with the following five leadership multiplier principles.

Chapter 11

The Watershed Moment of the New Testament

Multiplier Insight:
Calling

Autumn (Not Amazon) Prime

We have now reached autumn, the prime of Barnabas's life and ministry career. Larry and I intentionally chose the word *autumn* over *fall* for a few reasons. *Autumn* is the British word popularized by Geoffrey Chaucer (I was an English major) that captures the season between summer and winter. *Fall* describes the same season. It is a shortened version for "the fall of the leaf." *Autumn* is British, while *fall* is American. *Autumn* tends to be the more formal version of the word. We like the more formal version for our book. And when we hear the word *fall*, Larry and I theologically go to the second saddest chapter in Scripture, Genesis 3. (The saddest chapter is Jesus' crucifixion recorded in John 19.) So *autumn* it is. For our purposes, you can also think of the word *autumn* as synonymous with *prime*. Building upon spring and summer, by Acts 13, Barnabas has entered his ministry prime.

Larry and I both live in Los Angeles, the hype capital of the world. Film and television were born in our city and exported throughout the earth. One observation I have about Hollywood is that it is anti-aging. There is an obsession with youth. The younger, the better. I remember getting a haircut a few years back in a storefront strip mall. The woman cutting my hair began aggressively on my graying hair, "You have too much gray hair. You need to dye your hair." I told her that in the Bible, gray is good. She persisted, trying to upsell on hair color. I told her that in the Bible gray hair symbolizes hard-earned wisdom, righteousness, and guidance. I even shared Proverbs 16:31, "Gray hair is a crown of glory; it is gained in a righteous life." She fired back, "You have too much Bible!" I would contend that our culture has too much youth and world, lacking greatly in Kingdom wisdom.

As Barnabas begins his autumn season, he is likely in his late 40s to early 50s. During his church planting work at Lystra, the Galatians call Paul "Hermes" and Barnabas "Zeus" (Acts 14:12). Zeus is always portrayed in art as an older figure with white hair and a flowing white beard. Isn't it great news that the Kingdom of God is the opposite of the Los Angeles lifestyle? In LA, if you are in entertainment or sports, you are washed up at 35. But in the Kingdom, prime begins at 50.

The Church at Antioch

Antioch was founded in 300 BC by Seleceus Nicator, one of Alexander the Great's generals. He named the city after his father, Antiochus. Situated near the Syrian border in southern Turkey, the ancient city is known today as Antakya. The city was one of the jewels of the Roman Empire, the third largest city after Rome and Alexandria. It was known as "Antioch the Beautiful" because of its amazing skyline and long, paved boulevard. It makes me think of Rodeo Drive in Beverly Hills, Champs Elysees in Paris, and Nathan Road in Hong Kong.

During the first century, Antioch was divided into four quarters: Roman, Greek, African, and Jewish. Like many cities today, the cultural divides were strong. There was little cross-cultural activity among the quarters.

But two unnamed evangelists were so filled with the Holy Spirit that the message of Jesus crossed racial barriers. The city of Antioch, shocked by the multi-ethnic fellowship, were the ones to first name the disciples of Jesus "Christians" (Acts 11:26). After a year of preaching, teaching, and discipling, Barnabas built the first multi-ethnic church staff in history: Simeon the Black (African), Manaen (a slave of Herod's father), Lucius of Cyrene (Northern African), Saul of Tarsus (Asia Minor), and Barnabas (from Cyprus). This is the fulfillment of the Pentecost promise. In Jerusalem, they saw and heard the Spirit-fueled speaking and understood many languages. In Antioch, they lived out that multiculturalism on a pastoral team.

The church planting principle is clear: God's intended model is a multi-ethnic church. It has always baffled me why pastors stop at Acts 2 and crown the Jerusalem church as the model ministry. Jerusalem was the prototype. Antioch is the genuine article. The church at Antioch lived a powerful Gospel that transcended culture and launched every people group into discipleship and mission. When Paul teaches that there are no Jews or Greeks, I imagine he is thinking back fondly on what he learned at Antioch. Barnabas, the architect of the Antioch church, designed a model of church that we desperately need today. Now imagine being called to leave this church. Barnabas likely thought Antioch was his long-term ministry landing spot. But it was actually his laboratory. Everything changed for him at one of the all-time great prayer meetings.

The Spirit-Filled Prayer Meeting

The Acts of the Apostles can be divided into two sections. The first section (chapters 1-12) is the birth and growth of the Jewish mission. The central character is the apostle Peter. The second section (chapters 13-28) is the birth and growth of the Gentile mission. The central character is the apostle Paul. But there would be no Paul without Barnabas. Gentile church planting was born at the Antioch prayer meeting. This is why the great G. Campbell Morgan calls Acts 13:1-3 "the watershed moment of the New Testament."

The Lord Jesus loves to seek and save lost people. I think he loves to seek and save lost cities even more. How easy it would have been for Barnabas to grow the Antioch church into his own ministry empire. But the Father's will was to send out Barnabas and his charge as the first urban church planting missionaries. Barnabas and Saul were set apart to hand-deliver the Gospel to the lost cities of the Roman Empire. The first multi-ethic church plant was not intended to be a moment, but a model for urban missions. God brought the nations to the cities. Mission frontiers are no longer geographical. The barriers are cultural. The nations are down our street. Will we do the handwork of urban missions and deliver a Gospel that is good news, even across cultural lines? Barnabas and Saul were sent by the Holy Spirit into the heart of unbelieving cities.

The call to church planting came in the context of a church-wide prayer meeting. We know that when Barnabas and Saul returned from their first church planting mission journey, they reported to the entire church (Acts 14:26-27). This implies that the church as a whole, not just the five leaders named at the prayer meeting, set them off on mission. In an environment full of worship, the Holy Spirit speaks. The church is fasting. When we want to see God move, we pray. When we really want to see

God move, we pray and worship. When we are desperate to see God move, we pray, worship, and fast. The church was hungry for God and sought him, declaring he was more important than food. God did not disappoint. The command is quite vague. The details of their mission assignment are not disclosed. Sometimes we are on a need-to-know basis, and clearly, Barnabas and Saul did not need to know what they would do. This reminds us of Abram and Sarai's call (Genesis 12:1). The call to go is clear. The route or destination is not provided. This is a fresh reminder that sometimes a faithful response requires a flexible and brave spirit. I personally fear that our default today is strategy, not Spirit.

Dr. J. Robert Clinton defines destiny as "the formation process when God reveals his purposes for a leader in such a way that he inspires the leader to know his hand is on the leader's life." The year of church planting in Antioch could not have been easy. They were doing and learning ministry at a break-neck pace. There must have been more than a few sleepless nights where Barnabas and Saul wondered if they were on the right track. What validation it must have been to be set apart by the Holy Spirit! This is the third time Barnabas has been singled out in his mission development. He is chosen by the apostles to live into a new name (Acts 4:36). He is selected to investigate the new Gentile work at Antioch (11:22). And now he is chosen by the Holy Spirit to be sent out for urban church planting. The Antioch church laid hands and sent them off (13:3). The Greek verb for *go* can also be translated "let them go." The church at Antioch was trained well. Who were they to stand against God's destiny for Barnabas and his young protege? They understood that no single leader, even Barnabas or Saul, is bigger than God's mission. When Barnabas and Saul packed their bags and left the port of Antioch, church planting began.

Have You Read Page 111?

At age 30, Becky and I were sent out to plant a new campus ministry in the inner city. We moved to Long Beach and began a new work at Cal State Dominguez Hills and Compton City College. The ministry was exciting, challenging, and really beautiful. We thought we would continue to develop this campus work for the rest of our lives. But after a four-year cycle of campus work, the Holy Spirit gave us our next assignment in our larger call. On Monday, our ministry team discussed with our supervisor that God had put into our hearts the desire to church plant. On Tuesday, Becky and I met with a Christian businessman. When we walked into his office, he greeted us with "John and Becky, have you ever thought of planting a church?" Completely befuddled, we said, "Yes. Yesterday." We had no idea he was the bi-vocational executive pastor of a new church plant. On Friday, we had breakfast in Long Beach with church planting leaders from his denomination. The Holy Spirit was clearly moving. But what did it all mean?

The thought of leaving our campus ministry work was super scary. I became a Christian in college. Campus work was all I knew. Becky and I were comfortable and easily coasted. We were excited, confused by all these seemingly coincidental circumstances. In dire need of clarity we met for dinner with Bobby and Marilyn Clinton. As was always the custom, Bobby prayed and we paid. We asked Dr. Clinton one question, "How can we know the will of God with a really important decision?" We told him the story of our supervisor and two divine contacts in one week. Bobby put down his fork. He matter of factly stated, "It sounds like the Sovereign Guidance process item. Have you read page 111 of *The Making of a Leader?* That's how you discern the will of God." I absolutely love that Clinton memorized the page numbers of his own book. Who does that?[22] We smiled like we knew the page. He saw through my bluff. He pulled out a pen, and on the back of a napkin drew four quadrants to teach us how to discern God's will. The four quadrants were Bible and Spirit, trusted leaders, personal desire and current circumstances. We spent the next month seeking God in worship, prayer, and fasting. The Sovereign Guidance Decision Tool was such a timely grace for us. (Today it is one of the most-used tools in our ministry tool box.) We concluded with 87% certainty that God was indeed calling us out of our comfort zone to plant a new church.

Multiplier Insight: Calling

Barnabas models for us prime ministry achievements. The Lord set Barnabas apart for the massive tasks involved in church planting. Church planting and mentoring the younger Saul were two of his greatest contributions.

What if Barnabas and Saul did not worship, pray, and fast? What if they isolated themselves and blew off the prayer meeting? What if the church at Antioch said no to the Holy Spirit? What if Barnabas and Saul chose the comfortable and familiar and shrunk back from the risky and adventurous call?

Leaders who multiply embrace the fullness of their calling. Barnabas (and Saul) are models for us leaders today of what to do with our prime years. As you consider your prime, what massive Kingdom contribution did God call you to? What massive Kingdom contribution is he preparing you for?

---

[22] Author's Note: This decision-making process item is one of the three reasons I named my weekly newsletter "The 1-1-1." To sign up for my 1-1-1 newsletter, please visit johnteter.org/newsletter.

Chapter 12

Evangelism and the Forcefield of God's Word

Multiplier Insight: Evangelism

"The Holy Spirit Got Me!"

Most church planters say that evangelism is the primary reason they are starting a new church. I have yet to meet a church planter who shared, "God is calling me to start a church for stable Christians." The vision for new church planters is always evangelism. And in Acts 13, Barnabas and Saul show us how much we need the Holy Spirit to fulfill the hard work of witness.

In our first year of church planting, I was really struggling. The church plant was nowhere near where I thought it would be. I wondered if we made the right decision to leave our stable campus ministry. One Sunday afternoon, after a particularly discouraging Sunday, I drove home in the church U-Haul with my brother, Tim Sato. He could tell I was hurting. He asked what I thought of the service. All I could muster up was, "Well, we are one week closer to the Kingdom of God." He punched the gas a little harder after that comment. When we turned on our street, we were blocked by a 1980s Trans-Am (shout out to everyone who remembers the television show *CHiPs*).The Holy Spirit wanted to make sure we met the owner of this car. He was trying to park his Tranny when the engine died. He literally blocked our path. We hopped out of the U-Haul to help.

The first thing I noticed was a 14" T-knife tattooed on his arm. I asked him about his ink. He said, "I'm an urban chef." I later learned his parents were Mexican mafia, so his grandmother raised him. When he was a boy, every morning his abuelita would have three things on the kitchen table: flour for the tortillas, cocaine, and a gun. Granny was also a gangster, but she could cook. From an early age she instilled in him a love for cooking. When finishing up a stint in youth prison, he saw an advertisement for Le Cordon Bleu. He locked in and put himself through culinary school. When we met, he was an executive chef at a $50-per-plate fish house in Irvine, California. He said he had enough with the gun and coke. He was focusing on the flour.

Chef Mike and I became friends. He came over to our home and taught me how to make blackened fish tacos. His food burst with flavors. He took a step of faith and visited our core group Bible study, where 25 people gathered in our living room for inductive study of John 6:1-12. Chef Mike loved the feeding of the 5,000. As a chef, how could it be any other way? His first comment was, "I didn't know Jesus did catering events!" His next comment was, "I feed 100 people, and I am so happy. Jesus must have been the happiest person ever feeding 5,000." For three months Mike attended life groups and Sunday worship, bringing friends and family to church. When the time was right, we presented the Gospel. Mike said he really liked Jesus but was not ready to give up his old lifestyle.

On August 7, 2008, Chef Mike called me and left a message. It was the most glorious message. He said, "JT, call me. I became a Christian today. I was chilling in my room reading my Bible. It was blazing hot. The fan was on me. But then 'the Holy Spirit got me.' I surrendered my life to Jesus. Hit me back!" Fast-forward 17 years, and Chef Mike is one of the leaders in our church, a spiritual hero to many in our community. We were faithful in our witness. But it wasn't until the Holy Spirit "got him" that he became a disciple. Chef Mike Martinez is the first convert in our first church plant.

Evangelism and a Power Encounter

At this point, Barnabas and Saul had never heard a Gentile say, "The Holy Spirit got me!" They did not have a defined philosophy of evangelism. That would come later. They only knew the Holy Spirit sent them to cities in the Roman Empire that had no Christians. For Barnabas and Saul, evangelism was not an afterthought or a niche ministry. Without evangelism there would literally be no ministry. So they did the hard work of evangelism in Cyprus, visiting Paphos first.

Paphos was under the Roman governor Sergius Paulus. He set up a meeting with Barnabas and Saul. His office likely had more than a few complaints about these new missionaries proclaiming a new message in the synagogues. His official inquiry would help determine his course of action. He wasn't Jewish but probably felt the need to deescalate the situation to avoid further disruptions from his Jewish constituents. I wonder how Barnabas prepared Saul for the meeting. Did they have a specific Old Testament text they wanted to share? Did they consider tag-teaming as they presented the message to a high-ranking Gentile government official? Barnabas, Saul, and the governor could not have been prepared for what God had planned.

Luke describes Sergius Paulus as "an intelligent man"
(Acts 13:7, NIV). Because of his understanding and discernment, he was open to the message. But like most politicians, he had a shady crew of hanger-ons. A Jewish sorcerer and false prophet named Bar-Jesus was in the office that day. The dark arts of sorcery and magic were officially banned in Judaism, so he fled the region to set up camp in Cyprus. His Roman name was Elymas, which means "sorcerer" and "fortune teller." He probably saw an opportunity to drum up new business for his tarot card shop by quickly disposing of these two controversial Bible teachers. But Saul, a Jew named after Israel's first king, was also a Roman citizen. He likely felt super comfortable in the governor's hall. Elymas thought Saul would be a pushover. He could not have been more wrong.

As the Gospel was being proclaimed to Sergius Paulus, Elymas tried to block the apostle's message. We don't know whether he tried to cast spells on Saul and Barnabas, threw crystals at them, or physically covered the governor's ears. Luke only reports that he opposed the Gospel and tried to block the governor from becoming a disciple. Saul would have none of it. He turned on the sorcerer and pronounced a curse upon him. Drawing from the Hebrew language of the Old Testament, he called Elymas out as "a child of the devil," "an enemy of everything that is right," and one who is "perverting the right ways of the Lord" (Acts 13:10, NIV). Saul spoke blindness over him. Immediately, a mist and darkness covered the sorcerer. He began to grope about, seeking someone to lead him by the hand. In a moment of great irony, the sorcerer mirrors Saul's own conversion experience on blindness on the Damascus Road (Acts 9:8). Saul was blinded by the glory of the Lord. Elymas was blinded for blocking the glory of the Lord. Saul was taken by the hand to the house of the disciples. No one grabbed Elymas' hand, leaving him cursed, blind, and on his own. The governor, after seeing this miraculous display of power, believed in the Gospel message (Acts 13:12). Luke teaches that he was astonished at the teaching of the Lord. It was not just the message. The combination of the Word and God's power won him to faith. Barnabas and Saul must have been elated. When they left Antioch, the Holy Spirit did not tell them where to go. But clearly the Lord guided them to Cyprus, into the Roman hall of political power. The Holy Spirit broke new ground for church planting. They learned that power encounters on earth mirror conflict in the spiritual realm (Ephesians 6:12). The Holy Spirit gave Saul power to validate the preached message. Barnabas must have been so proud of how Saul was growing. The conversion of Sergius Paulus was a turning point in Saul's ministry, inaugurating a new ministry philosophy of direct evangelism to the Gentiles.

Word, Power, and Persecution

Barnabas and Saul's first encounter with the governor and the sorcerer provides the framework for their future church planting ministry: Word, power, conversion, division. Barnabas and Saul understood the centrality of God's Word in evangelism. They preached and taught God's Word. Barnabas was cut to the heart by Peter's first sermon at Pentecost. Saul was cut to the heart hearing the voice of the Word Become Flesh. Martin Luther made the Word of God the starting point and final authority for all under his spiritual care. He viewed the Word of God as "the all-powerful divine forcefield." I love how my friend and mentor Darrell Johnson puts it, "The Word of God not only informs, but performs, and ultimately transforms."

Barnabas and Saul would have loved ministering in our current environment. The unbelieving world today values experiential truth as much or more than propositional truth. There has never been a time in the history of the world when worldviews were up for grabs. In today's world, you can literally see people embrace a new culture, identity, friend-group, and even religion because of a person or experience. As urban church planters, we must use this for our advantage. Saul changed Sergius Paulus' worldview with one display of power. The power gifts (miracles, healings, word of knowledge, discernment of spirits) are meant to validate the preached message of the evangelist. In Jesus' evangelism conversation with the woman at the well, he delivered a word of knowledge, "You are right when you say you have no husband. The fact is, you have had five husbands, and the man you have now is not your husband. What you have just said is quite true" (John 4:17-18, NIV). Her testimony to the Sychar Village was not about the content of the living water (Word) but her experience of God's power. Her testimony brought the entire village to faith. The woman at the well *became* a well because of one word of knowledge.

When Barnabas and Saul entered a new city, Kingdom light and darkness separated. The men prayed hard. They preached hard. The Spirit authenticated their message. Everyone had a strong response. Jesus said it would be like this:

> "Do you think I came to bring peace on earth? No, I tell you, but division. From now on there will be five in one family divided against each other, three against two and two against three. They will be divided, father against son and son against father, mother against daughter and daughter against mother, mother-in-law against daughter-in-law and daughter-in-law against mother-in-law." (Luke 12:51-53, NIV)

Some, like Sergius Paulus, believed and became disciples. Some, like Elymas the Sorcerer, opposed the message and blocked evangelism. G. Campbell Morgan writes that evangelists must speak in love to Sergius Paulus while also speaking in anger to Elymas the Sorcerer.

The preached Gospel with authentication divides cities. Barnabas and Saul were loved by the believers. They were hated by the unbelievers. There was no in-between. I fear that most of us today live in the in-between. Sadly, I wonder if Barnabas and Saul would even recognize what we call evangelism today. They were direct in the presentation of the message. They were dependent on the Holy Spirit's power. Barnabas and Saul remind us that it is better to have 100 believers love us because of the Gospel than 10,000 people like us because we don't offend them.

Multiplier Insight: Evangelism

Leaders who multiply fully embrace the priority of evangelism. If you are gifted in evangelism, I pray you commit to turning your 10 talents into 100. The gift of evangelism is the first gift to atrophy and fall into disrepair. Use it or lose it. Be bold and lead the way for your church or ministry.

If you do not have the spiritual gift of evangelism, embrace the hard call of evangelism work (2 Timothy 4:5). Create a philosophy centered on helping people enter into the forcefield of God's Word. Like Luther, you will look back and declare, "The Word did all the work!"

As you preach, teach, and deliver the message, pray with confidence that God's power will validate your message.

Chapter 13

Family, Authority, and Second Chances

Multiplier Insight: Name, Family, and Mentoring

Family Matters

The first urban church planting mission team consisted of three people: Barnabas, Saul, and a teenager named John Mark. Barnabas's cousin is introduced as their "helper." The word in the original language carries the literal meaning of a synagogue attendant. Luke uses the same word for the man who handed Jesus the scrolls in his inaugural vision sermon (Luke 4:20). Many scholars believe John Mark's role was to care for the scrolls and record the mission journey. The young man started out documenting the church planting mission. I think it's fair to call John Mark the first church planting media artist. This falls into line with his communication gifting and how he would go on to become the first "viral" gospel author.

John Mark being Barnabas's cousin adds an interesting family dynamic to the first missionary journey. There are many who choose to avoid ministry with family. I have heard some go so far as to say that pastors shouldn't even have friends (let alone family) within the church they lead. But New Testament leadership is based on relationship. Of course, Barnabas would include his bright young cousin in his work. After all, John Mark's mother hosted the Last Supper, and John Mark was there with Jesus on the last night. Barnabas understood that friendships are both a ministry end and a means. The last chapter of Romans is evidence that Barnabas trained Saul to understand the same importance of ministry relationships. You cannot build healthy churches without healthy relationships. And if God has given you a family who are excellent Christian leaders, that is a special grace.

Becky and I have embraced church planting with our family. Our first church administrator was Carol Sato, my mother-in-law. Most people retire at 65 years old. Mom planted a church with us, serving as a world-class church administrator. In 14 years of service, she never dropped one ministry task. This freed Becky and me to do the hard work of evangelism: preaching, teaching, and developing leaders. My rule of thumb is that the more intense the ministry, the more we need family. I must caution that leaders who choose this model will be charged with nepotism. But the nepotism charge will not be an issue if the minister is a well-liked, respected servant leader. Barnabas poured into his family as he fulfilled his destiny to plant churches and develop Paul.

How Many Frequent Flyer Miles Would Barnabas Have Today?

The urban church planters set out for travel. But it was nothing like the common grace of travel we enjoy today. When they left Antioch, they sailed out of the port of Seleucia (modern-day southern Turkey) to Salamis, on the eastern coast of Cyprus. I find it so interesting that under the guidance of the Holy Spirit, they set up shop in Salamis, the most important city on the island. The trip was a 130-mile boat ride.

There were four travel options in the ancient world. Local seas were the most common ancient highway. King's Highways were land routes controlled by the nomads. Secondary systems were regional roads divided by the mountains. Long sea travel, such as their trip to Cyprus, was the major international crossroads. Ancient travel was full of peril. The first apostles had no luxuries, amenity kits, or flight upgrades. How many more churches would Barnabas and Paul planted with today's air travel? How many more books and letters would they have written collecting their thoughts in cars and Ubers?

Saul traveled over 10,000 miles proclaiming the good news of Jesus of Nazareth. His journeys on land and sea took him through present-day Israel, Syria, Turkey, Greece, and of course Rome. Some estimate, conservatively, that Paul would have needed at least 29 visas for his various church planting journeys. I wonder how many frequent flyer miles Barnabas and Saul would have had today!

When Saul Became Paul

A major shift in the mission team dynamic, and the history of the church, is sublimely introduced by Luke. From the first moment Barnabas and Saul are together, the team is always Barnabas first, then Saul (Acts 9:27). Barnabas, the encouraging exhorter, was deeply committed to Saul's development. He used all his early trust capital by putting his arm around Saul and affirming his conversion. No one else in the early church had that kind of trust with the apostles. He went on a long recruiting trip to Tarsus to recruit Saul, even though Saul had disappeared for over five years. Barnabas was the ultimate glue guy. He knew Saul was brilliant, gifted, and possessed massive Kingdom destiny. At Antioch, he designed an amazing team around Saul so that he could flourish. From the beginning, it was always Barnabas first, then Saul. Then they met the governor of Cyprus, Sergius Paulus (13:7, NIV). This moment was Saul's breakout. In NFL terms, Saul was the rookie wide receiver who delivered 200 yards and three touchdowns in a playoff game. There would be no turning back.

"From Paphos, Paul and his companions sailed to Perga in Pamphylia" (Acts 13:13, NIV). The reader who is paying close attention will notice two developments. The first is that the name *Saul* has been replaced by *Paul*. For the rest of the book, *Paul* is the exclusive name Luke uses for the great apostle. Saul is mentioned only three other times in Acts, each time in the context of recounting his conversion. Jesus and Ananias call him Saul. The name change is different from Barnabas's experience. The apostles changed Joseph's name to Barnabas to identify potential and set a high standard for spiritual giftedness. The apostles do not change Saul's name. Luke refers to him as Paul as a signal to the reader that this man has officially begun his Gentile church planting ministry. *Paul* is the Roman version of his Hebrew name, *Saul*. Because he is sent to the Gentiles, he embraces his Gentile name. For example, if God were to send me to the Chinese, I would adopt the name 约翰 (Yuēhàn). We must always present ourselves and our message so that our audiences can easily understand.

The second development is name order. My first job was as a file clerk for a business management firm that represented A-list Hollywood superstars. I remember a lawsuit against a production company because on the official movie poster, one actor's name was contractually to be placed before another. The case went all the way to the courtroom. Luke records the authority switch by now calling the mission team "Paul and his companions." By this point, Paul has become the leader to the point that Barnabas is not even mentioned by name. Barnabas's name is mentioned 22 times in the Bible. His omission in verse 13 speaks volumes. Paul is the leader of the mission team, and Barnabas willingly takes a step back into a secondary role. I think he is really pleased. The plan all along was to develop Paul.

Mentors love to see their charges surpass them. Leaders who multiply must choose to step aside and give younger leaders room to grow and maximize their full Kingdom potential. Barnabas, ever the encourager, does not call his lawyers, demanding justice (and the reprint of thousands of movie posters). Barnabas saw God move in power through his young protege. The spiritual authority of Paul far outweighed his own. It was time for the younger, more gifted leader to now be leading the mission. I bet Barnabas loved seeing Paul break out—but not everyone had the same perspective.

Scholars have long debated about why John Mark left the team at Salamis (Acts 13:13). If this happened today, the internet would explode with updates, reports, and even a few conspiracy theories. Scholars tend to fall into seven camps to understand John Mark left the mission:

- John Mark was young and homesick and wanted to go back to Jerusalem.
- John Mark was frail and ill and couldn't handle the physical challenges.
- John Mark was overwhelmed by the demonic realm and the spiritual power encounters.
- John Mark did not appreciate Paul and his hard-charging leadership style.
- John Mark was devoted to Peter and did not want to see Paul outshine his guy.
- John Mark did not agree with his cousin Barnabas submitting to Paul's leadership.

- John Mark was a more cautious person and feared for his
  life on the next leg of the mission.

As in real life, there is rarely a simple explanation for life-alter-
ing decisions. Why did a couple break up? Why did a senior in
high school choose one college over another? Why transition
from one job to another? It rarely boils down to one issue.
I believe John Mark left the team for a combination of two
reasons. First, John Mark was not happy with Paul's emerging
leadership. This is in stark contrast to Barnabas's maturity,
which ushered Paul to the next level. The evidence for this
is immediate context. Luke gives a not-so-subtle wink to his
readers by reporting on John Mark's defection immediately
following Paul's promotion to team leader. Barnabas proves
himself a world-class mentor in his reaction to the authority
switch. His mentoring work was almost complete.

The second reason is that John Mark was afraid for his life.
Evidence of this comes from his own writing. John Stott writes
that when John Mark left, he and Paul were headed to the
Taurus mountains. This rugged journey was dangerous. The
mountains were infested with pirates. Paul himself testifies about
the danger he experienced with bandits (2 Corinthians 11:26).
Those who have seen the film *Lone Survivor* with Mark Wahlberg
can understand why John Mark might be afraid.

John Mark confesses his own fear in the Gospel he penned.
Mark 14:51-52 tells of a young boy who was likely sleeping
when someone woke him to tell him Jesus had been seized
by the guards. He probably jumped out of bed, wearing his
first-century pajamas, and ran to Jesus. But at this stage of his
discipleship, he could only follow Jesus to a point until fear took
over. The guards seized Jesus. The guards seized the young man.
Jesus willfully submitted to suffering. The boy denied the cross
and ran away naked. The linen cloth symbolizes burial and the
boy running to save his life. Nakedness is always connected to

shame in the Bible. The young man was ashamed that he could not follow Jesus all the way to the cross, which begs the question of how John Mark could know such a private moment.

It is common among the biblical evangelists to record transactions in which they themselves took part without mentioning their own names. John is "the Beloved Disciple." Luke is "Lucius of Cyrene." The young naked man is John Mark. This is a confession of his discipleship weakness. The author dedicates a large unit of text to stress that disciples must choose faith over fear (Mark 5:1–6:29). John Mark ran in fear. It is no accident that the last word of Mark's Gospel is *afraid* (16:8). Fear was the character flaw in John Mark's life. The naked boy running for his life is his testimony.

We are all slow-growing disciples. We are not defined by one issue or challenge. Paul was young and had a short fuse. He probably confronted John Mark and called him a quitter. If young Paul was an NFL coach, "Next Man Up" would be the poster on his office wall. Yes, John Mark quit and caught the next flight home. Yes, he failed his first mission trip. But Barnabas never gave up on his cousin. I am so thankful for the mentors in my life who never gave up on me despite my many failures and flaws.

Multiplier Insight: Name, Family, and Mentoring

Leaders who multiply understand the priority and patience needed in mentoring. Those we mentor in our autumn season are like green, unripe apples. But with a little sun and water—and lots of time—they will become big, red, juicy apples. Barnabas, the encouraging exhorter, was full of grace and patience. What if Barnabas had given up on John Mark? Church history is super kind to John Mark. The long-term impact of Barnabas's mentoring is world-changing.

Who are the young Sauls you are mentoring, and what can you do to help them surpass you?

Who are the John Marks who need patience and prayerful processing from failures and flaws?

Chapter 14

The Five Functions of the Apostle

Multiplier Insight: Apostleship

Why Galatians Is the First Written New Testament Document

Paul and Barnabas were men who operated in the spiritual gift of apostleship. As a team, they first developed their gifts in the comfortable environment of Barnabas's home city. The team made the big authority switch to Paul's leadership (losing John Mark) as they moved their mission to Antioch Pisidia. In case you were wondering, there were many cities that contained the name Antioch in Barnabas's world. Seleucus, founder of the Seleucid Empire, named 16 cities after his father, Antiochus. Antioch Syria (Acts 11:19-30) is the mega city and launching pad for the Gentile church. But the journey to Antioch Pisidia was 100 miles through the North Mountains, which were full of violent bandits. At this second stop, Paul and Barnabas continued to grow in direct evangelism (Jew first, Gentile second), team dynamics, and persecution. This is where Paul preached his first recorded sermon. Paul and Barnabas further developed their apostleship gift by following the Holy Spirit into the cities of Iconium, Lystra, and Derbe (14:1-28).

As we've mentioned, Larry and I live in Los Angeles. The 405 Freeway is one of the most famous highways in the world. Three cities connect our two airports (LAX and SNA): Manhattan Beach, Long Beach, and Newport Beach. These three cities are independent but are part of Los Angeles. Iconium, Lystra, and Derbe are three smaller cities within the larger city of Galatia. So when you read Acts 14, you should also be reading Galatians (and vice versa). The reason Galatians is the first written document in the New Testament, even before the Gospel of Mark, is because Galatians was the first church plant. Paul wrote to the first church first.

Filled with the Holy Spirit and Good Works

Luke loves the theme of being filled. Consider how he repeats this theme throughout the book of Acts. The Holy Spirit filled the house of Mary, Barnabas's sister (Acts 2:2). The 120 disciples in the downtown Jerusalem apartment were filled with the Holy Spirit, and tongues of fire danced over their heads (2:3). The disciples were filled with the Spirit and began to glorify God in other tongues as the Spirit gave them utterance (2:4). In a moment of irony, the crowd comes to the conclusion that the disciples were filled with alcohol, even early in the morning (2:13). After Peter and John heal the lame man at the Beautiful Gate, the crowd is filled with awe (3:10). Under intense pressure during a trial, Peter is filled with the Holy Spirit (4:8). At the "Peter and John are in prison prayer meeting," all the disciples are filled to pray (4:31). Satan filled the hearts of Ananias and Sapphira to lie to the Holy Spirit about their giving to God's church (5:3). The authorities charge Peter and John with filling the streets of Jerusalem with the teachings of Jesus (5:36). (As a teacher of God's Word, should that same charge be our goal? What grace if one day I was charged with filling the streets of Long Beach, Compton, and Los Angeles with the teachings of Jesus!). Stephen, the Hellenist emerging leader is full of grace and power (6:8). Tabitha, the love-gifted evangelist is filled with good works (9:36). The Jewish rulers at Antioch Pisidia, observing all the converts to the way of Jesus, are filled with jealousy (13:45). The disciples in that same city are filled with joy and the Holy Spirit (13:52). This powerful theme of being filled continues through the rest of the book, but we will leave that for another time. Luke's message is clear. We will all be filled with something or someone. The opponents of God are filled with Satan and the flesh. The disciples of God are filled with the Holy Spirit and good works. And when we are filled with the Spirit, He will activate and develop our spiritual gifts. For Paul and Barnabas, this meant the apostleship gift.

The Five Functions of the Apostleship Gifting

"What exactly do apostles do?" Dr. J. Robert Clinton asked this question because the apostleship gift is one of the most controversial and misunderstood spiritual gifts in the New Testament. In a comparative study of the Acts of the Apostles, 1 Timothy, and Revelation, Dr. Clinton identified five core functions of the apostleship gift. Before we examine what apostles do, however, it is important to observe a characteristic of those who operate in apostleship.

Apostolic leaders are often multi-gifted leaders. The usual core combination is apostleship, teaching, and evangelism. These word gifts are the backbone of churches, so it makes sense that someone who starts a new church from scratch will need those gifts. This is a blessing, but there is a potential curse in abuse of power. Over the course of church history, false apostles claimed to be equal to the New Testament apostles. Some claimed God-given authority to write, and over-write, the Word of

God. I have yet to meet a contemporary apostolic leader who claims to write Scripture, but I am sure someone is out doing just that. The leader with the apostleship gift is often a strong leader with a very direct leadership style. Today's apostle often oversteps their gifting by abusing those around with a hard-driving, "my way or the highway" domineering leadership style. Complaints of force, manipulation, and other coercive tactics to gain compliance from followers fill the ministry of immature apostles. The healthy apostle must learn the hard lesson that self-awareness is not merely understanding ourselves, but being aware of how others experience us and our leadership. If you have the apostleship gift, being forewarned is being forearmed.

Now that we know some of the challenges and temptations of this spiritual gift, let's look at what apostles do.

Function 1: Praying and Fasting

The first function of the apostle is to pray. Apostolic leaders are called to intercede for ministries, new and old. Apostles, who are normally action oriented, must learn to seek God first on their knees. There is a unique spiritual burden and responsibility for the churches and ministries that apostles start, young and old alike. Those with the gift of apostleship must do the hard work of heavenly battle to begin and sustain their work. If God calls an apostle to a ministry, then you know he calls that apostle to pray for that ministry. Apostles, are you on your knees in prayer?

Function 2: Planting New Ministry

The second function of the apostle is to plant new ministries. The apostleship gift is synonymous with breaking new ground to establish new ministries. In Acts 14, Luke records how Paul and Barnabas inaugurate the church planting missionary movement.

The new ministries they plant deliver a fresh expression of Kingdom values. Power ministries of signs and wonders are often associated with planting new works. As God works through the apostolic leader, new followers will see God's work, sense the spiritual authority, and commit to build up the new works. The leader who operates in apostleship is not satisfied until the new ministry is established. Apostles, are you planting new works?

Function 3: Developing Leaders

The third function of the apostleship gift is the development of new leaders. At the beginning of Acts 14, Paul and Barnabas do the insanely hard work of starting a new church through evangelism. Over the course of the chapter, Paul and Barnabas use the powerful tool of modeling to grow and train their future leaders. At the end of the chapter, they strengthen the elders they have selected, trained, and appointed (14:23). Paul goes on to develop leaders on every missionary journey. Timothy appoints leaders in Ephesus. Titus appoints leaders in Crete. Apostolic workers must embrace the challenge to select, develop, and appoint leaders for new ministry. Leadership selection is the central message in Paul's letters to Timothy and Titus. New churches rise and fall on leadership selection. Apostles, are you developing leaders?

Function 4: Fighting Heresy

The fourth function of the apostleship gift is fighting heresy. On their return to Galatia, Paul and Barnabas encourage their leaders to continue in the faith (Acts 14:22). Luke uses the Greek word *emmeno*, which means "to hold fast, and remain in the proper place." Paul and Barnabas knew their young leaders were vulnerable to heresy, "an opinion or belief that is contrary

to orthodox doctrine." The Judaizers were trailing Paul and
Barnabas, trying to undo all the pure theology that had been
downloaded from the apostles. Heresy is like poison: 90% of the
combination is harmless, but that 10% will kill you. One of the
main points of the book of Galatians is to immediately reject
the heresy of the Judaizers. The Galatians started so well in
faith with Paul and Barnabas but were derailed by unorthodox
teaching. Apostolic leaders must combat heresy in their doctrine
(orthodoxy) and conduct (orthopraxy). This is why those with
the apostleship gift must always live in the Word. During seasons
of intense output and activity, the devil wants nothing more
than for the apostle to lose their theological edge. Apostles, are
you declaring war on heresy?

Function 5: Raising Funds

The fifth function of the apostle is resourcing the ministry.
Those with this gift have a special wiring and gifting to raise
money for new and existing works. In Acts 11 the Antioch
church, under the leadership of Barnabas, sends a gift to the
church in Jerusalem. Imagine the remote church plant sending
money so that the mother church can survive. It's a beautiful
moment of apostolic symmetry. Apostolic workers raise finances
for themselves, new ministries, and younger leaders. Apostles
must go the extra mile in personal and ministry financial
accountability. Abuse of Kingdom finances, which is quite easy
for apostolic leaders, is one of the six traps for those who do not
finish well. Apostles, are you raising funds for your ministry?

My Apostleship Hero

Robert Jaffray (1873–1945) is my apostolic hero. At age 20 at a
missions meeting in New York City, Jaffray answered God's call
to plant new ministries where Christ had never been named.

When Jaffray turned 24, he began his apostolic service by planting a new ministry in the Tung-Un region of Southern China. After 11 years, Jaffray learned a new language in order to expand the work to include the Indo-Chinese people group in Wuchow. He did the work of the apostle in Wuchow for 22 years. After a staggeringly successful apostolic career, Jaffray returned to the U.S. to supervise missions. But at age 55, the Holy Spirit gave Jaffray a later-in-life faith challenge. Jaffray accepted the call to plant a new ministry in Makassar, Indonesia. Jaffray would die in an Indonesian prison camp with many of the Christian leaders he brought to faith.

At the end of his life, Jaffray used his gifts to open three major ministry fields: South China, Indo-China, and Indonesia. He did the hard work of the apostle: praying with power, planting churches, training leaders, and fighting heresy where Christ had never before been named. Because he developed his apostleship gift, over one thousand new believers were brought to faith, four Bible schools for indigenous leaders were established, three printing press ministries were created, and the next generation of Chinese, Indo-Chinese, Cambodian, and Indonesian Christian workers were given a clear calling and path. I believe Barnabas and Paul will one day tip their hat to Robert Jaffray. Through many tribulations, Robert Jaffray entered the Kingdom of God.

Multiplier Insight: Apostleship

Leaders who multiply understand the true value of apostleship. If you are gifted in apostleship, I pray you turn your 10 talents into 100. Gift identification is never enough. We must do the hard work of developing that gift. How can you grow in praying with power, starting new ministries, developing leaders, fighting heresy, and funding the mission?

If you do not have the spiritual gift of apostleship, will you please pray for apostolic leaders? Apostles can be a handful. Healthy apostles are inspirational, strong, and help fulfill the Great Commission. But unhealthy apostles tend to build their own empires, reject accountability, and over-control those around them. Please pray for interdependence on healthy mission teams. God will hear your prayers for our apostolic leaders (Luke 1:13).

Chapter 15

Stones, Suffering, and the Thorn in the Flesh

Multiplier Insight: Suffering

The Man Who Stoned Stephen Is Stoned

In Acts 14, Paul and Barnabas planted the Galatian church by preaching the Word and performing signs and wonders (14:3). The church planting ministry in Lystra launched with a divine healing. Peter healed a crippled man in Jerusalem (3:1). Paul healed a crippled man in Galatia (14:8). The two miracle accounts are identical. This is Luke's way of reminding us that Jesus' prophetic vision (Jerusalem, Samaria, ends of the earth) was coming true. And it underscored the fact that Paul's spiritual authority was already equal to, if not greater than, Peter's.

The response of the Jerusalem Jews was persecution, leading to Peter and John's imprisonment. The response of the Lystra Gentiles was worship. The pagans thought Barnabas was Zeus, and they called Paul "Hermes." Our apostles quickly rebuked that Roman nonsense and insisted they were mere mortals who were filled with the Spirit of God. A hateful

Jewish mob from Antioch and Iconium began working the crowd. They convinced the crowd to hurl stones at Paul (for some reason Barnabas was spared). Paul was seized and held as the crowd hurled stones at his head. I wonder if this made Paul think about his role in the stoning murder of Stephen. He was dragged out of the city and left for dead. The murderers thought they had killed Paul. But the disciples who believed in his message gathered around him, prayed for him, and God restored him back to life.

In 2 Corinthians 11:25 Paul writes, "Once I was stoned." Can you imagine Paul's journal entry that night? "Today was crazy. I healed a crippled man who never walked before. The crowd then began to worship me. When I rebuked that nonsense, they grabbed me and stoned me to death. But God delivered me!" Luke writes that the next day Paul and Barnabas rose to make the brutal 60-mile journey to Derbe. If there was ever a time for a vacation, this was it. But Paul would have none of it. He got up and went to Derbe.

What Was Paul's Thorn in the Flesh?

I believe this section of Scripture sheds light on a burning question many have about Paul. What was his thorn in the flesh (2 Corinthians 12:7)? Three times Paul asks the Lord to take it away. I believe the evidence is found in the book of Galatians. This letter was written in 49AD, making it the first chronological book in the New Testament. Paul writes to the Galatians, "If possible, you would have gouged out your eyes and given them to me" (Galatians 4:15). Paul continues on that theme with, "See with what large letters I am writing to you with my own hand" (6:11). Why would the Galatians have offered to pluck out their own eyes and give them to Paul? Why does he have to write his letter in 50-point font?

The most reasonable answer is that Paul either lost or significantly injured one of his eyes in the Lystra stoning. He prayed three times that God would miraculously restore his eye. But the Great Physician, in his infinite wisdom, did not remove the thorn in his flesh. The Great Apostle was dependent on God, and likely his community, for the rest of his life. It is a severe symmetry that Paul was blinded on the Damascus Road, blinded the Jewish false prophet, but then lost his own eye to persecution. Paul's final words to the Galatian church were "I bear on my body the marks of Jesus" (Galatians 6:17).

Suffering and Sovereign Mindset

It must have been so difficult for Barnabas to see his friend and mentee suffer. Imagine the horror of Barnabas being held back, watching, as the crowd dragged Paul's dead body out of the city gates. How did Barnabas continue? How in the world did Paul get up and go to Derbe for more church planting the next day? The answer is that Barnabas and Paul lived with a sovereign mindset worldview.

"Sovereign mindset" is a fixed mental attitude of assuming God's gracious work in every activity of life. Barnabas had a predetermined mindset that God was at work in all of life's ups and downs, no matter the circumstance. Paul submitted to God's deeper purposes in life, even when it cost him his eye. Barnabas and Paul had strong learning postures, so they mined their own sufferings for invaluable lessons. The apostles never let their scars go to waste. They used them to bless those they led with hard-earned Kingdom wisdom. Rejoicing in their profound sufferings was at the heart of their spiritual authority. Their followers saw them bless God and continue to walk in faith in the face of absolutely awful circumstances. The hatred made them stronger. Paul and Barnabas knew that persecution and physical violence were part of God's sovereign plan for their development.

This mindset is clearly on display in the last third of the Acts of the Apostles. The prophet Agabus warns Paul with an object lesson of praying with his hands tied. He alerts Paul to future imprisonment if he were to return to Jerusalem. Paul goes on to declare in six of his letters that he is "the prisoner of the Lord" … except he is not. He is a prisoner of the Roman Empire. Why declare himself a prisoner of the Lord if he is in the custody of a Roman governor? It is a matter of perspective. Paul is under Rome's heavy hand of injustice, but he is supremely confident that God will use this for his good. No matter what Rome hits him with, he knows that God is at work to make him "more than a conqueror" (Romans 8:37). What does that mean? Conquerors are faster, bigger, smarter, stronger. They are the victors. In the short term, they are declared the winners. But someone who is more than a conqueror trusts in God and therefore turns the world upside down. They are slower, smaller, and weaker. In the short term, those who are more than conquerors lose. But because God works everything for their good, even when they lose, they win. That's the power of a sovereign mindset.

At the Third Beating, the Women Began to Weep

The physical suffering and the emotional trauma endured by Barnabas and Paul reminds me of the story of the Masai Warrior evangelist named Joseph. This story is shared by Michael Card:

> One day Joseph, who was walking along one of these hot, dirty African roads, met someone who shared the Gospel of Jesus Christ with him. Then and there he accept[ed] Jesus as his Lord and Savior. The power of the Spirit began

transforming his life; he was filled with such excitement and joy that the first thing wanted to do was return to his own village and share the same Good News with the members of his local tribe.

Joseph began going door to door, telling everyone he met about the cross of Jesus and the salvation it offered, expecting to see their faces light up the way his had. To his amazement the villagers not only didn't care, they became violent. The men of the village seized him and held him to the ground while the women beat him with strands of barbed wire. He was dragged from the village and left to die alone in the bush.

Joseph somehow managed to crawl to a waterhole, and there, after days of passing in and out of consciousness, found the strength to get up. He wondered about the hostile reception he had received from people known all his life. He decided that he must have left something out or told the story of Jesus incorrectly. After rehearsing the message he had first heard, he decided to go back and share his faith once more.

Joseph limped into the circle of huts and began to proclaim Jesus. "He died for you, so that you might find forgiveness and come to know the living God," he pleaded. Again, he was grabbed by the men of the village and held down while the women beat him, reopening the wounds that had just begun to heal. Once more they dragged him unconscious from the village and left him to die.

To have survived the first beating was truly remarkable. To live through the second was a miracle. Again, days later, Joseph awoke in the wilderness, bruised, scarred, and determined to go back.

He returned to his small village and this time, they attacked
him before he had a chance to open his mouth. As they
flogged him for the third and probably the last time, he
again spoke to them about Jesus Christ, the Lord. Before he
passed out, the last thing he saw was that the women who
were beating him began to weep.

This time he awoke in his own bed. The ones who had so
severely beaten him were now trying to save his life and
nurse him back to health. The entire village had come
to Christ.

Resurrection, Scars, and Kingdom Worship

In the Gospel of John, the resurrected Jesus appears to Thomas.
To convince his friend that the resurrection is true, he invites
Thomas to put his finger inside the wound. It strikes me that
Jesus is in resurrection mode. When Lazarus came out of the
grave, he was resuscitated. Lazarus had the same decaying
human body and would one day die again. But on Easter
morning, when Jesus came out of the grave, the only parallel is
when God created Adam and Eve. Jesus of Nazareth is the first
creation of "Humanity 2.0." Isn't it interesting that the body
that God the Son will have for billions upon billions of years is
scarred, wounded, and disfigured? In our perfected, resurrected
bodies, the scars from our gospel sacrifice will be clearly seen. In
fact, they will be celebrated. In Revelation 4, the host of heaven
worships God the Father and declares that He who sits on the
throne is "Holy, Holy, Holy." In Revelation 5, the host of heaven
worships God the Son and declares that he who was slain
(heaven sees his wounds and scars) is "Worthy, Worthy, Worthy!"

This section (Acts 11:19–14:28) ends with a triumphant return
to Antioch. Imagine the worshipful reflection as they sailed back
along the Mediterranean coast. The international pastoral staff

team of Simeon the Black, Manaen, and Lucius of Cyrene
must have wept for joy when Barnabas and Paul returned.
The church at Antioch must have been filled with faith as they
heard how God answered their prayers for the first church
planting team. The worship service must have gone far into
the night as they described how God had opened the door of
faith for the Gentiles (14:28). And everyone must have freaked
out, and probably had to look away, when they saw Paul's eye
and disfigured body. Paul lived his own teaching, "We must go
through many hardships to enter the kingdom of God" (14:22).
The apostle gave his eye, but like Barnabas when he first arrived
at Antioch, Paul saw the grace of God.

Jesus' scars are celebrated in heaven. Barnabas and Paul's scars
are celebrated in heaven. Joseph, the Masai warrior's scars,
will be celebrated in heaven. Your scars, and my scars, will be
celebrated in heaven. But pity upon so-called disciples who have
no scars.

Hast Thou No Scar?
by Amy Carmichael

Hast thou no scar?
No hidden scar on foot, or side, or hand?
I hear thee sung as mighty in the land,
I hear them hail thy bright ascendant star,
Hast thou no scar?

Hast thou no wound?
Yet, I was wounded by the archers, spent.
Leaned me against the tree to die, and rent
By ravening beasts that compassed me, I swooned:
Hast thou no wound?

No wound? No scar?
Yet as the Master shall the servant be,

And pierced are the feet that follow Me;
But thine are whole. Can he have followed far
Who has no wound nor scar?

Multiplier Insight: Suffering

Leaders who multiply have embraced the value of suffering. Barnabas and Paul were able to rejoice in their sufferings because of their sovereign mindset. As his autumn season came to a close, Barnabas would need a sovereign mindset. There was no way he could be emotionally prepared for his next ministry challenge.

WINTER

*"Winter is on my head, but eternal spring
is in my heart."
— Victor Hugo*

Winter is not the season of endings—it is the season of
enduring influence. In the agricultural world, winter is when
the soil rests, the roots deepen, and the hidden work beneath
the ground determines the harvest of future generations. The
winter season in the life of a multiplier is the same. It is the stage
when the leader's greatest fruit often grows indirectly, quietly,
and through the lives of others. This is the season Robert
Clinton calls the "afterglow"—the phase in which a lifetime
of character, wisdom, and perspective begins to shine through
leaders who have learned to empower, release, and bless the
next generation.

Robert Clinton describes the afterglow as the culmination
of decades of God's shaping. It is the season when a leader's
ultimate contribution emerges—not through position or
platform, but through spiritual authority, generational investment, and the willingness to "hand off the baton" with grace.

My winter started at age 64 when, after 31 years, I transferred
leadership of our church and took a unique role of national
leadership in our denomination. Leaving the pastorate changed
my life dramatically, and although I was not done, I was
different. I was influential but not necessary.

Winter leaders no longer measure success by what they
personally produce but by what flourishes in those they have
influenced. Their voice is quieter, but their impact is deeper.
Their schedule is lighter, but their wisdom is heavier. Their days

are slower, but their legacy accelerates. A winter leader's mantra is simple: "How do I help the mission outlive me?"

No biblical figure captures this winter posture better than Barnabas. After the public spotlight shifts to Paul, Barnabas steps into his afterglow season—less visible in the narrative of Acts, yet more generative in his impact. He becomes a bridge between Jewish and Gentile believers in moments of tension. He takes John Mark under his wing when others dismiss him. He returns to Cyprus to strengthen the churches he helped start. His name fades from center stage, but his fingerprints remain everywhere—on Paul's ministry, on Mark's Gospel, on Antioch's sending culture, and on the unity of the early church. Barnabas finishes well not by doing more, but by multiplying deeper.

Winter is the season where a multiplier turns their attention to legacy, spiritual grandchildren, and the future of the mission. It is the invitation to invest in emerging leaders, to capture and codify life lessons, to serve as a sage rather than a star, and to shift from "leading the team" to "blessing the next generation of leaders." It is a season not of withdrawal but of repositioning, not of retreat but of release. The winter leader discovers the holy joy of seeing others surpass them, of watching new ministries rise, and of knowing that God has used their lifetime to shape people who will impact the world.

This section of the book invites you into the beauty and responsibility of the winter season—the season when God does some of his finest work through leaders who have nothing left to prove, nothing to protect, and everything to give. Barnabas shows us that the final decades of a multiplier's life can be the most fruitful of all, not because of what they do but because of who they empower.

Chapter 16

Advancing Your Bullet Points

Multiplier Insight:
Essential

Multipliers declare, defend, and delight in the essentials of the Gospel. They prune the distractions of non-essential issues.

On January 1 I will climb a mountain … in the dark … again. I will climb to a place where I can see for miles in many directions. After digging a seat in a snowbank and laying down my big black garbage bag over the snow, I will sit down and wait. As I wait, I will pull out my journal and begin to renew my identity, reviewing the essence of who I am, and recommitting myself to my essentials.

As the sun rises on the first day of the next calendar year of my life, I will be singing worship to Jesus. I will surrender myself to my Lord and dedicate the new year to his glory.

I will look back on the previous 365 days and give God my gratitude for his grace and faithfulness. I dream forward, envisioning what I would believe God to do. I will recenter my life around what matters most to me, my essentials.

This has been my spiritual ritual since I hit my 60s, my winter season. I have less and less time for anything but my most important values. I'll strip my life back down to my beloved basics. This is how you "win your winter."

The Essentialist Wins the Championships

"Gentlemen, this is a football." These were the opening words of the 1961 Green Bay Packers training camp as Coach Vince Lombardi held up a pigskin ball. It wasn't sarcasm; it was conviction. The Packers had suffered a heartbreaking loss at the NFL championship in 1960. Coach Lombardi believed it was due to a neglect of the basics of football.

For that entire camp he stripped it down to the essentials, the fundamentals of football. He famously declared: "If you can't block and tackle, you can't win." Some of the players grumbled, but Lombardi stuck with the essentials. The results were undeniable. From 1961 to 1967, the Green Bay Packers won five NFL championships in seven years, including Super Bowls I and II. Lombardi's teams were not known for gimmicks or complex strategies. They were famous for execution of the essentials.

As I travel the nation speaking to pastors, so often I want to hold up a Bible and say, "Friends, this is a Bible" or "This is the Gospel" or "This is discipleship." Nothing fancy, no cool AI-enhanced presentation, no complex strategy to reach lost people. Just the simple, essential, fundamental but also powerful, life-changing, movement-starting truth.

Winter strips things to the bare essentials—like trees. In the winter season you clarify what the main things really are. You prune non-essentials activities from your ministry life. Multipliers keep the main thing the main thing. They pass on passion, not for programs but for the Gospel.

You get clear on what you want your life to multiply. The message of your life gets clear.

The Essential Dogmatist

Barnabas was around 60 years old when Acts 15 kicked off his winter season. At this point, Barnabas was not deciding what he would give his life to. Instead, he was looking back over what he had given his life for. He was not done yet, but he was praying about how to finish strong and to pass on as much of his gospel passion as possible.

Paul and Barnabas had just returned to their home church of Antioch from their approximately 18-month missionary trip of 1,300 miles. They had experienced miracles, conversions, persecution, and new churches starting. But as they are rejoicing, some troublemakers come to Antioch from Judea. They are teaching a supposedly "higher form" of Christianity, one that requires not only faith in Jesus but also the covenant and act of circumcision. These teachers insist this act is an essential for salvation.

Barnabas is usually Mr. Diplomat, but here he becomes Mr. Dogmatic. He and Paul have a "heated argument and a strong debate" with these false teachers. Barnabas knows that the essential truth is being attacked. The Gospel of salvation in "Christ alone, by grace alone, through faith alone" is in jeopardy. This is a battle worth fighting. This is worth gripping so tightly that only death could pry your fingers loose of these essential truths.

A Few Glass Balls

Three decades ago I heard a life metaphor that impacted me. I saw a juggler who could juggle nine balls at a time. Five of them were rubber, and four were glass. As he juggled, he would say, "This is your life. You are going to juggle many different balls in life, and sometimes you are going to drop balls. The rubber balls will bounce back. The glass ones won't. To live a good life, know the difference and don't ever drop the glass ones."

Barnabas knew the Gospel was a glass ball. If he and Paul compromised the message of grace, the pure Gospel would be poisoned. They were willing to walk 300 miles to Jerusalem to debate this in front of the Jerusalem elders. The text implies that their defense of the Gospel was both theological and biographical. They defended the message they had been preaching AND they reported the signs and wonders being done in the Gentiles in response to the message.

Their vigorous testimony and the testimony of Peter led to a decision that protected the Gospel and liberated the Gentiles. They would not be bound by the law of circumcision. If you were there you probably heard some "Hallelujah!" shouts from Barnabas and Paul.

Barnabas helped keep the Jewish religious culture from compromising the purity of the Gospel. Likewise, you must discern when cultural baggage is blocking the view of grace. Culture needs the discernment of the Holy Spirit. Often culture needs to be adapted to. Barnabas did that when he went to Antioch the first time (Acts 11:22). But culture also needs to be dissected from the unchanging bottom lines of the Gospel. Barnabas also did that in Antioch when he brought back the letter from Jerusalem (15:31) and then stayed there to teach them more of the Word (15:35).

In the winter season more than ever, you must distinguish between the main things and the minor things. At this age you must be done with dabbling in and debating the minor topics that distract from the purity and power of the Gospel.

Older Fire

God gave a command that is important for all of us, but especially winter leaders. Leviticus 6:12 says, "The fire on the altar must be kept burning; it must not go out. Every morning the priest is to add firewood" (NIV). God ignited the fire in Leviticus 9:24 and, at least symbolically, it burnt for centuries until 586 B.C. when Babylon destroyed the temple. Spiritually that fire was rekindled in the upper room at Pentecost when a fire came into the room and then distributed itself to the head of everyone there.

How old is a fire that has been burning for years? It's the same fire (in this case ignited by God himself) but fed fresh fuel daily so that it's burning like a new fire. Mid-life crises or the loss of passion as we age often causes people to seek new fires to try and get the "zip" of life back. The solution is not a different fire but putting fresh fuel on the same fire.

Multipliers grow more excited about the essentials the older they get. These essentials are not stale head knowledge they can lecture others on. They are truths that bring fire to their bones and set others who get close to them on fire.

Multipliers experientially understand that "we teach what we know, but we reproduce who we are."

How contagious is your current gospel potency? Get honest by asking yourself these questions:
- How fresh and alive is the Gospel for my own life today?

- Do I still find God's grace to be amazing?
- Is the Word alive and vibrant to me?
- Is making disciples who make disciples the most compelling and thrilling part of my life?
- Is my prayer life a living conversation with Jesus?
- Is the old gospel story what I am most excited to share with new people I meet?

Bullet Points

Neil Cole taught me about bullet points. Many years ago I was listening to the legendary multiplier teach. At one point he got super serious and slowly stated, "My life is centered on a few bullet points. My bullet points are a few truths in life that matter so much and that I believe so deeply, I would take a bullet for them."

In winter, life begins to strip you down and reveal what your bullet points are. Bullets kill, but we all should have bullet points that make us more alive, that we are willing to die for.

A few months ago, I was in impoverished Togo, Africa, spending three days teaching 25 Christian leaders from 11 different countries. A brother named John came in from northern Nigeria despite having been beaten nearly to death for the third time for preaching the Gospel. He was one of the most alive men I have ever met. I was humbled to spend time with him. I wanted to tell him, "John, don't go back," but John knew his bullet points. The gospel essentials were his life and joy.

The Prison of Preferences

In winter, your comfort zone is more tempting. It's cozy there. Leaving it becomes more and more difficult. The "new" doesn't do it for you like the "old" used to—the new worship songs, the new preaching style, the clothes the worship leader wears, the screens that make it look like a theater, the AI-enhanced sermons.

This calls for a different kind of discernment, one that distinguishes between content and form. One that prioritizes substance over style. One that recognizes the difference between cultural adaptation and gospel alteration, between preferences and convictions.

Juanita Moore was a 75-year-old saint in our church when I arrived to pastor Light & Life church. She'd been sitting in the same pew singing the same hymns for three decades. As I began to change the worship style, some of the older folks began to leave because we no longer sang enough hymns. I had disrupted their comfort zones.

I went to Juanita and asked her, "Juanita, are you thinking about leaving like several of your friends have?" She answered, "Not at all, pastor. I don't like this new music at all, but people are getting saved in our church now. And I like seeing people getting saved a lot more than I dislike the music. That's what we're really here for!"

Juanita was a Barnabas. She would have been gone in a minute if we twisted the truth of God's Word. But changing the worship music? Not her preference, but the essentials mattered so much more. Juanita refused to get bogged down in trivial matters when the vital matters needed all her energy. What preferences or distractions are keeping you from investing energy in your essentials?

One-Year-Old Wood

Winter is the season for pruning. Vines are pruned down to their essentials. In the world of viticulture, pruning is often described as the most important task of the year. If you left a grapevine to its own devices, it would grow into a tangled mess of wood and leaves with very little (and very sour) fruit.

Perhaps the most important reason for pruning is that the fruit grows only on one-year-old wood. This is the most critical biological fact about grapes. Old wood (older than a year) will never produce fruit; it only produces more wood. New green shoots (this year's growth) produce the fruit, but they only grow from buds that formed on last year's wood. Consequently, if you don't prune, then the "fruiting wood" moves further and further away from the trunk every year, eventually leaving you with a huge vine that has no grapes near the center. Pruning brings the fruiting potential back close to the "heart" of the plant.

Multiplier Insight: Essentials

Leaders who multiply major in the majors. As Christian leaders, if we hope to multiply disciples, leaders, and churches in our winter years, we must keep pruning our lives back to the spiritual essentials. We stay "young at heart" and "contagious in spirit" when we prune the distractions and dead wood in our lives. We focus on the trunk of our lives and believe for fresh "one-year-old wood" experiences where the new fruit will grow.

Chapter 17

Changing Up, Not Out

Multiplier Insight: Transitions

Multipliers surrender transitions to the Lord for gospel advancement and courageously embrace new multiplication opportunities.

If you are 62 today and you are a male in the U.S., you are expected to live another 20 to 23 years. Ladies, you get an extra 3-4 years for having to put up with us guys for so long. So here's the question, how are you going to live 20+ years of your life? How fruitful will your winter be?

The median retirement age in the U.S. is between 63 and 65. For clergy, it tends to be two to three years later. How do you view retirement? Should Christian leaders actually retire? The winter season of leadership brings life's most challenging transitions. How we navigate those transitions determines our late-in-life impact and how well we finish life and ministry.

As Barnabas enters into his winter season, he is approximately 58-60 years old. He is likely martyred at 65-70 years of age. These 10 last years of his life will bring several transitions. Acts 15 describes many of them.

But Barnabas changes up not out! He doesn't retire; he repositions. He walks through these transitions with the heart of a multiplier. He's not power- or position-hungry. He's convinced that making disciples and leaders who reproduce other disciples and leaders is the most effective means of building the Kingdom.

Four transitions Barnabas made that most leaders must make during winter:

1. A change from spotlight to acting coach

Barnabas had been the star of the show, as he was esteemed in Jerusalem then the leader the apostles sent to Antioch. He was the golden boy. He was the key leader of the Antioch church as it flourished and grew. He wasn't asking for the spotlight, and he proved that by going to get his mentee Saul to help with the ministry in Antioch. Nevertheless, the spotlight kept shining in his direction.

As they were sent out as a mission team, Barnabas's name was stated first and Saul's was second (Acts 13:1, 3). But the order changed along the way (13:42, 43, 46), and by Acts 15 they were "Paul and Barnabas." However, when they came to Jerusalem for the council, Barnabas is momentarily listed first again (15:12, 25). Why? Probably due to the context of the audience. Among the Jews in Jerusalem, Barnabas was still the big man on campus.

Then in Acts 15:35, when they return to teaching the Antioch church, it's back to "Paul and Barnabas." When they were planning the mission to return to the churches they had started, it was Paul who made the final decision about which partners would be going.

Barnabas goes on a mission to Cyprus and sails off the pages of the New Testament. He moves from the spotlight to a backstage acting coach. He transitions away from the Broadway stage of Jerusalem, Antioch, and a world tour and to the off-Broadway of comparatively small Cyprus. Once there, church tradition tells us Barnabas became a "father of a movement," the culmination of ministry dedicated to multiplication.

This reduction in work, titles, positional authority, and notoriety is a common kind of winter transition. There comes a time to give up the main stage. It's much better to *walk* off the stage than to be carried off. Too many pastors overstay God's assignment and confuse stepping aside with stepping out.

Here are common justifications from pastors who delay or refuse transition:

"If I'm not the pastor here, who am I?" (identity confusion)

"No one will need me once I step aside." (codependency)

"I can't afford to leave—even if I wanted to."
(financial bondage)

"There's no one ready—and I'm protecting the church."
(successor failure)

"We can't imagine this church without you." (pastor centrism or ego)

"This is the last thing I still control." (power loss)

"Leaving would mean quitting." (mission confusion)

"I don't know what I would do next." (calling misunderstanding)

"What if it all falls apart after I leave?" (false responsibility)

It's difficult to hear the Spirit inviting you to your next assignment when fear of transition is hissing in your ear. The winter season tempts you to think, "I'm done." But as the song "My Testimony" declares, "If I'm not dead, You're not done. Greater things are still to come. Oh, I believe."[23]

The Hand Off

When I was 62, I heard the Lord clearly say, "You need to hand the church off to younger leadership within the next two years. If you stay longer, I will do good things for a time, but you will 'hobble' the next generation of leaders and the future of the church." I had led the church for 30 years and was still energetic and effective. I had no other ministry position lined up at that point. But Deb and I were determined to obey the Lord, and we enacted a two-year succession plan. It culminated in the church leadership being handed off to two co-lead pastors who were in their mid-30s. I was 64. That was four years ago, and every year since, Light & Life has had a record number of baptisms at the church.

Today I have a winter position, not retired but repositioned. Serving with no staff, no assistant, no office, no office hours, no structured schedule, and no authority—but significant influence. I have been empowered as part of our denomination's National Leadership Team to seek to instill a culture of multiplication in our churches nationwide. I am starting to experience winter firsthand.

---

[23] Elevation Worship, "My Testimony," track 5 on Graves into Gardens, Elevation Worship Records, 2020, streaming audio, accessed December 21, 2025,

The key to transitioning well through this repositioning change
will be woven through the rest of this book. Suffice it here to say
that Barnabas did it beautifully, and we can learn from
his example.

2. A change in key ministry partners

Barnabas and Paul were great friends and powerful ministry
partners. Barnabas was a mentor to Paul. Then they were
friends for approximately 12 years and ministry partners for
about 7 years. Imagine having a friendship where there is
mutual admiration, a passionate love for Jesus, a love of God's
Word, and a common missionary calling. Then have that friendship sail the seas, hike hundreds of miles, camp out frequently,
confront sorcerers, observe miracles, see mass conversions, and
start churches. These brothers were tight! They were PB&J:
Paul, Barnabas, and Jesus!

But even great friendships and ministry teams often change over
time. Barnabas and Paul could not agree on the mission team
for their next trip. Paul said, "No way" to taking John Mark
with them because he had deserted them on their first trip.

Paul was prioritizing mission reliability, mission stewardship, and
consequences for past failure. Paul probably expected people
to persevere at the same level he did. Barnabas was focused on
Mark's potential, long-term Kingdom usefulness, and redemp-
tive second chances. The fact that he was Barnabas's cousin
may have contributed as well.

Paul and Barnabas were debating mission strategy and best
team members. They disagreed, but it doesn't appear that there
was a fracture of their relationship. Luke never describes this
separation as relationally broken. For Luke—who *does* name
relational failures elsewhere—this silence matters. Later Paul
mentions Barnabas with respect, esteem, in public, and as a
peer (1 Corinthians 9:6). In addition, Paul's later recruitment of

John Mark to minister with him is a significant statement about the nature of this disagreement.

Nevertheless, it had to grieve Barnabas that his mentee would actually feel so strongly about this that he would split up the partnership. Have you ever had a mentee who ended up ditching you, disagreeing with you, or connecting with a different leader than you? Ouch, right!?

Healing Your Heart

Relational pain in ministry is reality. Don't assume that because you are in winter all your relationship conflict is behind you. Barnabas is a model of experiencing relationship pain in winter but not letting it defeat him.

If you do ministry right, you cannot escape this kind of pain. You must love deeply enough that if ministry calling separates you from a ministry partner, it hurts … really hurts. That hurt can take you one of two places: self-protection or the cross. You can pull back your heart, become invulnerable, trust less, and fly solo more OR take your pain to the cross and claim the healing that flows from the vulnerability of Christ. Real love took Jesus to the cross, and that's where it will take you too. His healing will keep your heart soft because only then can you give it away.

In winter you can be tempted to think back on all the relational hurts and goodbyes and decide, "I am done with giving my heart away." The only way to transition healthily is to grieve the loss, release the past, be healed and filled by the Spirit, and start ministering again with new partners. Start new mentoring relationships.

If you don't embrace this transition, you will be stuck in your memories instead of living in your possibilities.

Think like a multiplier. Although Paul and Barnabas split
up over the choice of ministry partners, there is good reason
to believe they ended up rejoicing over the multiplication of
ministry teams! Team one: Paul and Silas. Team two: Barnabas
and Mark. Impact doubled. My guess is that they blessed each
other's teams before they departed.

Multipliers are always looking for the "Kingdom win," even
when the multiplication arises out of disagreement.

3. A change in ministry location

The median tenure of a pastor is about eight years. The average
pastor will lead three or four churches over a career of 35 years.
Your ministry can never be defined by your current location.
Barnabas started in Cyprus, ministered in Jerusalem, led in
Antioch, traveled in mission, and then in his winter season he
returned to Cyprus for his final years of ministry.

The winter season often brings a geographical transition.
Leading reasons for relocation include family proximity
(those grandkids), affordable living (or am I just talking about
California!), climate or health considerations, giving the new
pastor space (especially in smaller towns), your spouse's desire
(after all, they followed you for decades), and new ministry roles.

Barnabas probably chose Cyprus because it was home. He still
had familial and spiritual networks of relationship there. It was
an ideal place to mentor John Mark. Barnabas went back to the
work he had pioneered with Paul. He went home to ensure that
what already existed would endure. It was also a smaller, safer
space, and given Barnabas's advanced age, travel on one
island nation would have been much easier than what he had
been enduring.

Whatever the relocation reason, this transition is significant.
Often leaders are limited by their locations. Multipliers,

however, see relocation differently. They are not looking to make a big splash in their new place. Instead they are looking for individuals to disciple and potential leaders they can pour themselves into to launch them to their next level of ministry.

4. A change in ministry rhythms

For nearly 30 years I preached three or four times every Sunday. Sabbath was Monday. Staff was Tuesday. Midweek was Wednesday. Small group was Thursday. Then I hit winter, and I repositioned. I went to Cyprus, still in ministry but a very different rhythm.

Now I usually don't preach on Sundays. I spend two weeks a month traveling to speak, teach, attend meetings, or lead conferences. I have no office and no set hours. I have no staff and no assistants. I work remotely. I Zoom a lot. My favorite thing is discipling individuals. Suffice it to say, my rhythm is very different. I'm on Cyprus time.

One of the blessings or banes of the winter season is that generally your time becomes less structured. But without imposed discipline, leaders often end up wasting much of their time in winter. A few examples from winter leaders I know:

- Failing to replace external schedules with internal rhythms and focused mission, creating days that just blur together
- Measuring today against how it "used to be"
- Becoming stuck in unhealthy nostalgia instead of using healthy remembering to fuel the future
- Being a critic of those who don't do it like you once did
- Overconsuming—whether it's food, news, social media, movies, games on your apps, sports, hobbies, podcasts, etc. (These become time-fillers but not Spirit-fillers.)
- Disengagement in terms of isolation or volunteerism, an "I've done my time" attitude

Barnabas didn't retire to this island in the Mediterranean to get a suntan, sip umbrella drinks, and improve his golf game. He invested his time for Kingdom advance, but he did it at a different pace than previously. Multipliers use their winter pace to go narrower and deeper with a few who will take the Gospel further.

Multiplier Insight: Transitions

Leaders who multiply learn to leverage their transitions. Multipliers face each transition with questions like:
- "How do I use this new reality to become more like Jesus?"
- "Will I let my prior reality keep me from fully engaging in my new reality?"
- "Will I try to stay visible—or am I willing to stay fruitful?"
- "Will I explore the joys and multiplication possibilities of my new reality?"

Our answers to these questions determine whether we move from "strength to strength" (Psalm 84:7) with each new transition and keep multiplying.

Chapter 18

Investments That Pay Off Big

Multiplier Insight: Investments

Multipliers intentionally invest in themselves and in leaders who will multiply.

When I was in my late 20s, I told someone I invested $7,000 in a new car. I found out I was wrong. A financially wise person schooled me: "It's not an investment if it depreciates. Investments appreciate. Expenses depreciate." I knew what he meant, and it was basically true. A more accurate statement would have been: "Investments create future value. Expenses are consumed with no enduring return."

The Season of Withdrawals

Winter, however, seems to focus on withdrawals. You withdraw from your 401K, Social Security, IRA, savings account, insurance policy—even the piggybank in your closet.

You withdraw from your marriage account. If you have invested wisely over the years, your last season will be rich with laughter and love. My wife and I do marriage seminars and often share this truth: Consider your marriage like a house. Every investment you make in your marriage is building and decorating that house. It's the house you will live in until you die. Are you building a house you will be happy to live in?

You withdraw from your health account. All those workouts during your first three seasons mean something important during your final season.

You withdraw from your friendship account. I got a card on my 68th birthday from my best friend of 42 years. Dwight's card read, "It takes a long time to grow an old friend." We are enjoying skiing, biking, boating, serving, and traveling together in our winter.

The bottom line: Invest wisely over the seasons so you can withdraw richly during your winter. You will do winter wrong, however, if you don't keep investing. Winter will reveal your former investments, but it will also require new investments if you want your life to multiply and have maximum impact.

Barnabas may have withdrawn from Antioch and Paul's missions team, but he did it so he could invest in Cyprus and in John Mark. He didn't go to Cyprus on a cruise or vacation or move to his retirement home. He went to invest himself in mission, in something that would increase in value after his departure. Although Barnabas fades from the pages of Acts, there is some Scriptural evidence for what was happening during his winter years. Other thoughts can be surmised from how Barnabas had lived up to this point and where that trajectory would most likely take him during his final season. Still other winter glimpses may be distilled (with abundant scrutiny) from second through sixth-century church fathers and Church traditions. Some of the material from here forward will draw from these sources.

Your Four Big Investments in Winter
(and every season!)

When I was 12, I took a marker and carefully wrote Luke 2:52 on an index card: "And Jesus increased in wisdom and in stature and in favor with God and man." Underneath, I inscribed: "To be the best man of God I can be in all areas—Mental, Physical, Spiritual, Social." I taped this to my bathroom mirror and remind myself daily, "Larry, this is who you want to be." It stayed there for the next 35 years. I would see it whenever I returned home, and it would spur me on in the right direction.

Now in my wintertime, I am committed to these same four commitments. Dave Ferguson calls them "RPMS," and Exponential uses them as a framework to encourage healthiness in leaders:

R – Relational Investments: Deepening old friendships and making new friendships is one of the joys of the winter season. Your time is more flexible, allowing for more time to invest in the right friends.

It is "not good for a man (or woman) to be alone" at any age, but especially during winter.

Social isolation among those 65+ increases risk of premature death by ~30%, dementia by 50%, heart disease by 29%, and stroke by 32%.[24] The better friendships and family relationships you build, the better your health will be.

P – Physical Investment: Often my body says, "Take it easy. You've been exercising for 60 years. You've earned the recliner life." It's a lie that goes against your created design. "Motion is

---

[24] National Academies of Sciences, Engineering, and Medicine. (2020). *Social isolation and loneliness in older adults.* Washington, DC: National Academies Press.

lotion" is a mantra I repeat to myself to get me going. The body is made for movement.

Did you know muscle tissue is trainable into your 90s? Sarcopenia is the progressive, age-related loss of muscle mass, strength, and function. It increases the risk of weakness, falls, and loss of independence—especially when movement and strength training are neglected. It happens to everyone, but it can be thwarted.

If you invest in nutrition (especially plenty of protein), good sleep, some kind of cardio exercise, and resistance training two to three times a week, you will see the dividends. It's a spiritual matter because your body is HIS temple, and you can't let pigs make their home there.

M – Mental Investment: Leaders are learners … until they stop. Many leaders have been learners because of their careers instead of being motivated by their curiosity. Curiosity is a key to winning in winter.

Research consistently shows that curiosity in later life is associated with slower cognitive decline, greater mental flexibility, and lower risk of dementia-related symptoms.[25] The brain ages fastest when it stops being invited to wonder.

The aging brain still grows when it's challenged, not merely occupied. Read demanding books (biography, theology, history—not just news or fiction). Take a class (online or local) that stretches your thinking. Learn a new skill or hobby or game. New learning forms new neural connections—even later in life.

---

[25] Sakaki, M., Yagi, A., Murayama, K., Robertson, E. M., & Takeuchi, H. (2018). Curiosity in old age: A possible key to achieving adaptive aging. *Neuroscience & Biobehavioral Reviews*, 88, 106–116.

The mental investment includes understanding your mind and emotions. Daniel Goleman, author of the classic *Emotional Intelligence* (EQ) often talks about emotional literacy—learning to recognize, name, analyze, then respond (not react) to what you are feeling. This self-awareness is the cornerstone of EQ. Winter will present many emotional challenges, but investing intentionally in your emotional health will help guard your heart with the peace of God.

S – Spiritual Investment: Investing in spiritual depth is assumed in winter, but it shouldn't be. Many leaders find that much of their spiritual life has been driven by ministry roles and tasks. Winter should give increasing space for practicing spiritual disciplines for the joy of them, pursuing the Lord for the pleasure of his presence rather than the help you need for Sunday's sermon, feeding on the Word just to feed your soul rather than feed the church.

The richness of the relationship you have built with Jesus is what you will enjoy and grow during this season. If you find that relationship lacking, it is not too late to form a more intimate one. Try these:

- Linger in prayer with more questions and more listening.
- Remember treasured memories with joy and thankfulness.
- Meditate on Scripture as a love letter from the Father for this season of life.
- Try new spiritual disciplines you've neglected over the years.
- Enjoy more times of solitude just being still and receiving the Father's love.
- Identify the worship music that feeds you and moves you and feast on it. Find new artists.
- Explore new forms of worship and new genres of worship music.
- Form friendships with those who want to talk about Jesus and have deep conversations centered on him and his Word.

Multipliers Invest in Developing People

As you follow Barnabas's life through Scripture, there are multiple places where we can either postulate or clearly state that he was investing in making disciples and leaders:

- In Jerusalem, for approximately 10 years after his conversion, he probably served as a house church leader, disciple-maker, house church planter, leader of leaders (Acts 4–9).
- In Antioch he taught, led, and discipled other leaders there for one to two years (Acts 11:26).
- On his first church planting journey with Paul, he preached and taught for about two years (Acts 13, 14).
- Upon their return to Antioch, he and Paul spent one to two years teaching and leading (Acts 14:28).
- Following his defense of the Gospel in Jerusalem (Acts 15), he spent approximately one year teaching and discipling in Antioch.
- His ministry with Mark in Cyprus lasted three to eight years.
- After Mark, Barnabas was sent to minister with Paul (5-10 years, to death).

Making disciples, mentoring leaders, and raising up church planters was Barnabas's ministry priority throughout his life. There is then no doubt that this pattern continued upon his return to Cyprus with John Mark. Barnabas invested his winter season in making disciples, mentoring leaders, and apprenticing Mark.

The winter season usually means a shift from platform to people, from speaking at gatherings to conversing with individuals. Winter provides more personal disciple-making time. All Christians for all of their lives are called to obey the Great

Commission of going and making disciples. Retirement doesn't cancel this assignment.

Multipliers Invest in Discipling, Mentoring, and Coaching

In our winter season, our investment in people has fewer distractions. Free of office hours, budget meetings, busy speaking schedules, staff management, etc. we can give ourselves to more life-on-life engagements.

A point of clarity is helpful here. Leaders often get hung up on the differences in discipling, coaching, and mentoring. Different people have different definitions for each of these. Becoming bogged down in semantic differences is unhelpful—just invest Jesus into people. The truth is, all three overlap. At the same time, I *do* find it helpful to see the distinctions between these terms. It helps clarify the relationship.

Discipling

Discipling at its root level means "forming a person in the way of Jesus." (We are never commanded to "mentor" or "coach" others, but we are called to "disciple.") Disciple-making is an active verb. It is a holistic process that includes everything from salvation (reaching the lost) to maturation (growing the believer) to multiplication (the disciple making another disciple).

Multiplicative disciple-making includes five essential elements:

Relational – life on life, not just information; a brother or sister for life

Scriptural – grounded in and immersed in the Word of God, knowing it and loving it

Spiritual – teaching a reliance upon the power of the Spirit and the power of prayer

Accountable – focused on obeying Jesus to become more like Jesus

Reproducible – targeted toward the goal of the disciple making a disciple

Although I am now actively involved in a national leadership role, my greatest ministry joy has come from my frontline discipling. Greg, one of my disciples, was quarterback on my high school football team and is now a contractor in Kansas. Greg was "a religious do-gooder who went to church sometimes" (his words). After 45 years we reconnected, and Greg met Jesus for real and caught the Spirit's fire. I have been discipling him for three years now. A couple of weeks ago, Greg asked me if I could join a Zoom he was having. He wanted me to meet some of my "spiritual grandchildren." I got on that call with five other dudes from Kansas, and each one gave his testimony. Some even told about who they were now discipling. During that call, Greg stated in amazement, "I knew I could build pulpits, but I never knew I could build people."

Leaders who keep deeply discipling will find a flow of living water filling them and flowing through them. Disciple-making is a grand adventure where Jesus shows up big.

Mentoring

Mentoring can be summed up as "sharing wisdom from lived experience," which leads to the core question: "What have I learned that might help you?" Unlike disciple-making, mentoring does not require a whole life commitment. You can mentor others in certain areas and for specific periods of

time. It is rooted in your life experiences, your education, your
opinions, and your wisdom.

Mentoring seeks to share perspective, context, insights,
discernment, and inspiration. It is often story-based, allowing
real-life stories to carry life and vocational wisdom. Mentees are
learning how to thrive in their gifts and calling, so mentoring
is good listening, sharing your journey, imparting insights, and
offering prayer and love. In short, it's being a Barnabas (son of
encouragement) to others in ministry.

Every week Deb or I is asked by a younger leader, "Can you
mentor me or point me to someone who can?" There is a
dearth of older leaders stepping up to say, "I want to mentor
some younger leaders." Yet one of the greatest joys of your
winter season can and should be pouring your wisdom into the
next generation. It's a bit like being a grandparent in that you
can love them, tell them stories, then hand them back and say,
"I'm here if you need me."

Help them move forward in the season they are in. This is
multiplication work.

Coaching

Coaching is not about shaping identity or discerning calling; it is
about execution and skills. Along your journey you have picked
up skills that you probably use without thinking. However, most
of those skills are not being taught to younger leaders. They've
got the heart, but these leaders need some training so they don't
have to live in the "school of hard knocks," as my dad called it.

Younger leaders want to gain insights into questions like:
- How do you decide when "good enough" is good enough?
- How do I lead people older or more experienced than me?

- How do I know when to push for results versus when to be patient with people?
- How do you form a bold but wise budget for the church?
- How do I confront a board member who is gossiping?

Coaching is an investment in the effectiveness of leaders and will live on after you're gone.

Multiplier Insight: Investments

Leaders who multiply prioritize investing in leaders or leaders to be. They understand that discipling forms the soul; mentoring shapes the journey; and coaching accelerates growth. You can coach skills and mentor leaders—but you disciple souls. All three have a high ROI (return on investment), and they are the joyous work available to all winter leaders.

Chapter 19

Designing Your Legacy Today

Multiplier Insight:
Legacy

Multipliers focus on ultimate contributions that will outlive them, even if their name is not attached.

Anna and Susan Warner were multipliers, the only civilians to ever be buried at West Point. Not politicians. Not donors. Not famous leaders. Just two unmarried sisters who loved Jesus and who, like Barnabas, discipled and encouraged others, especially the young cadets at West Point.

For over 40 years (including through their Winter season) they held Bible studies in their home near West Point. Their meetings focused on Scripture study, discussion, prayer, and character development. Their home was a place of refuge, calm wisdom, and sincere love.

Their influence on West Point was profound. Their disciples went on to be generals, chaplains, and national leaders. They wrote books, poems, and songs about Jesus—including one of the most renowned songs in Christianity, "Jesus Loves Me."

The Warner sisters left a quiet but powerful Kingdom legacy that continues to this day.

Legacy Defined

Legacy is the transfer of conviction, wisdom, and spiritual DNA into people and systems that outlive the leader's authority and presence. In the context of multiplication, legacy is not what people remember about a leader, but what continues to grow because of them.

This is why your real legacy won't be known until you are gone. Many unknown Christian leaders will end up having much more significant legacies than many better-known leaders who were content with large but shallow results.

If we were to recount Barnabas's legacy it could include: 1) legitimizing Paul, 2) helping establish the Antioch church, 3) launching the first intentional missionary movement, 4) helping plant churches across Asia Minor, 5) raising up church elders, 6) defending Gentile inclusion in the Church, 7) defending the Gospel of grace, 8) restoring and training John Mark, 9) establishing and strengthening the church in Cyprus, and 10) making disciples wherever he was.

What do these 10 accomplishments have in common? They continued after Barnabas was dead. They multiplied in some way. They did not require living in the spotlight.

As described earlier, Barnabas's winter season embodies what Clinton calls afterglow—a phase where formal authority diminishes but influence continues through people. Scripture offers no record of Barnabas reclaiming center stage after Acts 15, yet his legacy surfaces later when Paul himself affirms Mark as "helpful" for ministry (2 Timothy 4:11, NIV). This delayed fruit underscores another Clinton insight: many leaders never see the full extent of their influence in their lifetime.

Barnabas's winter legacy was carried not through titles, roles, or institutions but through transformed lives—proof that leadership influence is transmitted primarily through people, not positions. Barnabas finished not loudly, but faithfully with his fruit growing on other people's trees.

In John 15 Jesus didn't just encourage us to bear fruit for him. He had a certain kind of fruit in mind: "fruit that will last," legacy fruit (John 15:16, NIV)! The only way to make an apple really "last" is to plant the seed and grow an apple tree that will bear more apples with more seeds. This is the power of multiplication. This is why, in Genesis 1, God emphasizes seed-bearing plants. It is also why God's first commandment is, "Be fruitful and multiply." This is what would fill the earth with his people.

I was humbled, and legacy was clarified for me through an experience I had after repositioning (which I shared in detail in my book *River Church* but which bears repeating here).

Forgotten?

On January 9, 2022, after 31 years of pastoring, Deb and I handed the leadership of our church to two sons in the faith. We stepped away for seven full weeks. When I returned, I slipped into the 9 a.m. service alone and a little early. A greeter I'd never met smiled and asked, "Is this your first time here?" I smiled back. "No, I've been a few times."

Inside, an usher—also unfamiliar—asked if he could show me a seat. For 31 years I'd sat on the front row, same spot. I assumed I might still land nearby. Instead, he led me to one of the worst seats in the middle of the row and asked cheerfully, "How's this?" I nodded. "Perfect." Then he added confidently, "You're really going to like the preaching … now."

I sat there quietly fuming. *Lord, I gave my life to this place. Seven weeks gone, and no one knows my name.* The Lord's response was gentle but piercing: *Was it ever about your name?*

During worship, I sensed him saying, *Look at the front row.* There sat my two sons in the faith leading the church. Beside them were leaders they had discipled—and next to them, people those leaders were discipling. The Lord whispered, *That's your legacy. Generational disciple-making and leadership empowerment. People may forget your name, but they will live for mine.* That's fruit that lasts.

The Four Big Legacy Moves

As leaders move deeper into the winter season, the question quietly but insistently changes. It is no longer "What can I still accomplish?" but "What will continue when I am gone?" Winter strips leadership down to its essentials. Energy narrows. Authority diminishes. Visibility fades. What remains is legacy.

Legacy is not accidental. It is shaped—often most decisively—when leaders stop expanding their influence and start "transmitting it." In this season, four contributions matter most: 1) a successor, 2) spiritual children, 3) churches, and 4) resources. Together, they form a legacy that does not depend on presence, personality, or position.

1. A Successor: The Courage to Prepare Someone to Replace You

The most obvious—and often most avoided—legacy contribution is a successor. Winter exposes how deeply a leader trusts God. Preparing a successor requires confronting mortality, irrelevance, and the temptation to remain indispensable. Healthy winter leaders do not merely name a successor; they create one.

I am often asked, "Can you help me find a church planter or successor?" I usually say, "No, but I can help you raise one." Multipliers give away authority early, publicly bless emerging leadership, and resist the urge to hover or compete. They understand that succession is not about preserving personal preferences, but protecting mission continuity.

In a sense Barnabas had two successors. The first was his mentee, Saul/Paul. Barnabas had a secure position with the Antioch church, but he went looking for Saul. He helped Saul into leadership in the church. He was raising up someone who would surpass him in impact and authority. As their mission trip progressed, Barnabas gracefully and humbly handed off leadership. For multipliers it's about Kingdom expansion, not position entitlement. Paul was a part of Barnabas's legacy. How enthusiastic are we about handing our authority, credibility, and ministry over to successors who might surpass us?

His second successor was John Mark. After Mark's failure on their first trip, Paul was adamant that he would not go on their second one. Barnabas was committed to seeing Mark invested in and restored. Consequently, Barnabas took Mark to Cyprus to minister. For the next 7-10 years Barnabas spent as many as 10 of his winter years mentoring Mark. Barnabas's anointing and mantle are passed onto Mark. This was not a positional succession but a spiritual one.

Instead of taking leadership in Cyprus, Mark returns to the mainland and is recruited by Paul to join his ministry. Colossians 4:10 (NIV) is remarkable: "My fellow prisoner Aristarchus sends you his greetings, as does Mark, the cousin of Barnabas. (You have received instructions about him; if he comes to you, welcome him.)" In 2 Timothy 4:11, Paul is even clearer: "Get Mark and bring him with you, for he is very useful to me for ministry." These verses reveal that Mark is now a trusted coworker with Paul, moving freely within apostolic networks and considered reliable enough to be sent independently. Mark is a coworker with Peter, who also commends Mark by calling him "my son" (1 Peter 5:13).

This vindicated Barnabas's investment in this next generation leader. His winter years were well spent in ways that left a powerful legacy.

2. Spiritual Children: Investing Your Friendship and Wisdom

Not every leader will name a formal successor, but every multiplier will leave behind spiritual children.

Many of my "winter" friends in Christian leadership tell me the same thing: "What I like most about this season is my chance to spend more time with my kids and grandkids." The same is true with spiritual children.

Spiritual children are those who look to us as spiritual parents. They have a special relationship with us that has been shaped by our spiritual influence in their lives. They carry our spiritual DNA. They are passionate about what we are.

Earlier seasons favor breadth—more people, more influence, more reach, bigger platforms. Winter favors depth. High-impact leaders expend their time in fewer but deeper relationships with younger leaders.

Spiritual children often carry a leader's legacy farther than successors because they are not tied to a single role. They infiltrate many leadership contexts with Jesus' love. They multiply. Many winter leaders underestimate how powerful this contribution can be simply because it is so hidden.

My wife has done hugely fruitful ministry over her 50 years of ministry. Dr. Deb has served on the frontlines in urban North Long Beach and Compton, California. In her winter season she (at 66 years old as co-pastor) and I handed off the church. She thought she was "aging out" and expected to see her impact decrease. Instead, she found herself on the National Leadership Team of our denomination. Her position carried no authority, no staff, but significant influence and freedom to lead as she saw fit.

Never one to sit in board meetings, she decided she was going to give her best efforts to doing what she called "leader discipleship" with younger female leaders. For the past four years, she has invested a year of mentoring in 12 to 25 key leaders. Best of all, the requirement for being in her group is that they will multiply and do the same with other female leaders. Her "spiritual children" are now having a significant impact on our denomination. Her winter has turned into the most influential season of her life.

During his winter season the apostle John wrote, "I have no greater joy than to hear that my children are walking in the truth" (3 John 4). We will not all have children or grandchildren, but we can all know the joy of raising up spiritual children!

3. Churches: Strengthening a Community That Outlives You

Our church is 72 years old. It has had 10 pastors over that time. Eight of those pastors are now in heaven, yet the church lives on. My 31 years of pastoring were built on their legacy. My two spiritual sons are powerfully leading the church now, and I pray she is here long after I am gone. Most of your local churches will live on in some form after you die. Jesus clearly stated the one thing he was building on earth: the Church. Jesus, through the local church, is the hope of the world.

According to church tradition, Barnabas spent his winter season strengthening the local churches of Cyprus. With no official position or ecclesial authority, yet with the credibility built on a lifetime of ministry experience, he encouraged, taught, and blessed churches.

Too many Christian leaders greatly diminish their commitment to their local churches during their winter because they are no longer leading positionally. Our legacy is not what we leave that has our name on it. Neither is it only the individuals we influence. It is also the churches we strengthen.

Winter leaders can redefine success in ways younger leaders often cannot—yet. Encourage church metrics to shift from size and speed to depth and durability, from addition to multiplication. Affirm disciple-making and leadership development. Normalize seasons of pruning, rebuilding, and slow growth. What you celebrate shapes what the church pursues.

This kind of legacy is rarely celebrated. Strengthening churches does not produce immediate metrics. It does not generate headlines. But it produces durability—and durability is the true test of legacy.

Another part of personal legacy may be using our winter wisdom to serve on boards of Kingdom-building organizations that will endure past our lives. Deb and I both serve on different boards that are directly helping build the church.

4. Resources: Capturing Wisdom for Individuals and Generations You Will Never Meet

Winter leaders increasingly recognize resources —books, courses, letters, frameworks, and digital tools—as vehicles of legacy. Speaking ends. Writing endures.

Barnabas left no written texts we can trace directly, yet his influence survives because others preserved what he modeled. Because of his mentoring, teaching, and encouraging role with Paul, there is undoubtedly some of Barnabas in each of Paul's epistles.

As John Mark's primary mentor, Barnabas had a profound influence on the Gospel that Mark wrote. Without Barnabas's restoration of Mark, it may not have been written. Most evangelical scholars also believe that Luke's writing was significantly influenced by Mark's Gospel. So Barnabas's influence, if not his words, were recorded in the words of others and lived on.

Leaders need to do the hard work of organizing and packaging a lifetime of ministry insights, wisdom, and resources. The biblical letters are a great example of tools given to younger leaders for fruitful ministry. What are you writing today that those who come behind you will find helpful?

Every winter leader needs to write a book—not with the goal of selling copies or becoming a famous author, but with the aim to distill, share, and preserve the learnings of their life. The process alone is invaluable to your soul. You have wisdom to transmit to the next generation.

Multiplier Insight: Legacy

These four contributions—successor, spiritual children, churches, and resources—work together. No leader will emphasize all four equally, but every leader should intentionally invest in more than one. Together they answer the winter question: "What will continue without me?"

Leaders who multiply understand these four dimensions - A successor ensures continuity of leadership. Spiritual children ensure continuity of values. Churches ensure continuity of mission. Resources ensure continuity of wisdom. These create a rich legacy.

Legacy is not what people say when you are gone. Legacy is what they are able to do because you were alive. This is the work of a multiplier in winter.

Chapter 20

The Well-Finished Life

Multiplier Insight: Finishing

A multiplier has a clear definition of and a holy dedication to "finish well."

One third, 33%. Based on Dr. Robert Clinton's qualitative, longitudinal analysis of biblical, historical, and contemporary leaders, only one third of Christian leaders "finish well."[26] Sadly, I don't need the research to know this is true. I am watching it happen.

The Winter Passage

As Deb and I entered our winter season, we determined we would "finish well." The first thing we did was to memorize Psalm 92:12-15 and make it our theme:

> "The righteous flourish like the palm tree and grow like a cedar in Lebanon. They are planted in the house of the

---

[26] Clinton, J. R. (1988/2012). *The Making of a Leader: Recognizing the Lessons and Stages of Leadership Development*. Colorado Springs, CO: NavPress. See also Clinton's Leadership Emergence Theory lectures and research summaries.

LORD; they flourish in the courts of our God. They still bear fruit in old age; they are ever full of sap and green; to declare that the LORD is upright; he is my rock, and there is no unrighteousness in him."

Our passion is to finish well, to live the words of this psalm. To Deb and me this means:

- To flourish in life ("like the palm tree")
- To keep growing ("like a cedar")
- To stay planted in the Church ("house of the Lord")
- To stay engaged in the Church ("flourish in the courts of our God")
- To keep producing Kingdom impact ("still bear fruit")
- To stay fresh, vibrant, curious, and young at heart ("ever full and green")
- To stay on message! God is right, and God is Good! ("The Lord is upright")
- To find our solidity not in circumstances but in God ("he is my rock")
- To live holy lives ("no unrighteousness in him")

By following these principles from Psalm 92 we want to make our winter as rich as possible!

Barnabas's Eulogy

Barnabas's gravestone could have had these words engraved: "He was a good man, full of the Holy Spirit and of faith. And a great many people were added to the Lord." Those exact words were used to forever testify to Barnabas's life and ministry in Acts 11:24.

Luke likely wrote Acts around AD 62–64, when Barnabas was at his finish line, near death. This means Luke's description of Barnabas is a retrospective, a considered judgment written nearly two decades after the events it describes.

Acts 11:24 reads like a eulogy more than a résumé. David Brooks wrote, "There are two sets of virtues: the résumé virtues and the eulogy virtues."[27] The résumé virtues are the accomplishments, positions, and skills you bring to the job market. The eulogy virtues are the ones people will talk about at your funeral—whether you were kind, brave, honest, or faithful.

About 300 years after Barnabas, another Christian leader ministered in Antioch: John Chrysostom. He had an incredible résumé, which led him to become the Archbishop of Canterbury. Yet his life and preaching emphasis was always the "eulogy virtues." Chrysostom said, "It is not the greatness of our actions but the goodness of our lives that makes us pleasing to God."[28]

Defining Finishing Well

Paul knew he was near death. His legal case was finished. Nero was a madman. Paul knew his beheading was coming soon. So, he looked back and declared his final testimony: "I have fought the good fight, I have finished the race, I have kept the faith" (2 Timothy 4:7). But Paul also focuses forward: "Now there is in store for me the crown of righteousness, which the Lord, the righteous Judge, will award to me on that day—and not only to me, but also to all who have longed for his appearing" (2 Timothy 4:8, NIV).

---

[27] Brooks, D. *The Road to Character*. New York: Random House, 2015.

[28] John Chrysostom, *Homilies* (4th century). Paraphrase reflecting Chrysostom's consistent teaching that the goodness of one's life, not the scale of one's actions, is what pleases God.

Finishing the fight. Finishing the race. Finishing faithful—but also anticipating with joy receiving the award the Lord has for those who love him. This is finishing well.

Through comparative studies of hundreds of leaders, Dr. Robert Clinton identified a set of six common characteristics demonstrated by those who finish well. Most effective finishers exhibited at least four or five of these six traits.

1. A vibrant relationship with God: They continue to cultivate spiritual intimacy with God. They live out of a deep well of the Spirit. Jesus is their first love.

My daddy died when I was two, so death had a significant place in my young mind. I can remember being 7 years old in my bedroom kneeling down and asking Jesus if my last words on earth could be, "I love you, Jesus." I guess I figured that would be a good note to finish on. I still believe that.

2. A lifelong learning posture: They keep growing. They maintain what Stanford researcher and professor Carol Dweck calls "a growth mindset." This humble and hopeful approach keeps people learning. It reframes setbacks as learnings, not failures.

These "finishers" keep seeking wisdom. Proverbs 8:34-35 underlines the life found in wisdom seeking: "Blessed are those who listen to me (wisdom), watching daily at my doors, waiting at my doorway. For those who find me find life and receive favor from the LORD" (NIV).

Oscar Wilde once quipped that "Wisdom comes with age, but sometimes age comes alone." Aging is automatic and happens quicker than we imagined. As columnist Jennifer Yane insightfully stated, "Inside every older person is a younger person wondering what happened."[29] Wisdom is not automatic. It must be pursued daily. We must wait daily at her door.

3. A Christlike character: "To be like Jesus, to be like Jesus, all I ask, to be like Him. All through life's journey from earth to glory, all I ask to be like Him." Some, especially those in winter, started humming, singing, or hearing a melody in your head. Why? Because this simple chorus has been sung at camp meetings, revivals, and altar calls for the past one hundred years. Its simplicity captures the earnest plea of those who really know Jesus and want to live and finish well.

If you want a clear picture of Jesus, just imagine the fruit of the Spirit perfectly exhibited: "love, joy, peace, forbearance, kindness, goodness, faithfulness, gentleness, self-control." Pursuing the growth of these character traits must be a lifelong quest.

After studying thousands of leaders, Clinton wrote, "God is more interested in developing the leader than in developing the leader's ministry."[30] Finishing well requires that a leader's inner life (character) has kept pace with or surpassed their outer life (accomplishments).

4. Truth lived out (conviction in action): Leaders who finish well possess convictions that have been tested by suffering, refined by obedience, and integrated into daily decisions. Truth lived out shows up in private, not in sermons. Truth known is doctrine. Truth taught is ministry. Truth lived is character.

---

[29] Jennifer Yane. (n.d.). Quoted aphorism on aging and identity, widely attributed to Yane in cultural discussions of aging. The statement reflects Yane's recurring theme that personal identity often remains internally youthful even as the body and circumstances change.

[30] J. Robert Clinton, *The Making of a Leader: Recognizing the Lessons and Stages of Leadership Development* (Colorado Springs: NavPress, 2012), 13–14.

Leaders who finish well have personal stories of how God's promises and truths worked in every season. Winter strips leaders of positions, roles, platforms, and applause, leaving only their true convictions. Consistency between belief and behavior builds a legacy of authenticity.

In 1980 Eugene Peterson wrote his seminal book, *A Long Obedience in the Same Direction—Discipleship in an Instant Society*. In it, he consistently warns that ministry can deform the soul of leaders who confuse success with faithfulness, substitute busyness for obedience, and trade depth for visibility.[31] Deep and slow seems antiquated. Yet shallow and fast leaves us vulnerable to an emaciated inner life where our convictions don't reach the core of our being. Those who finish well live and minister from the inside out.

5. Lasting contributions (legacy): Those who finish well typically leave behind one or more ultimate contributions in their lifetime. They made an impact that will outlive them. This could be a ministry they built, a church they led, disciples or leaders they mentored, publications or ideas they contributed, or any meaningful work that endures. Effective finishers don't just drift into retirement with nothing to show; they maximize their latter years to solidify a legacy. They can point to something tangible that God accomplished through them for his Kingdom that remains as a testament to their life's work.

David exemplifies finishing well. He sinned horrifically at mid-life, but he repented deeply and kept pursuing God. In his winter season he prepared materials for building the temple (an ultimate contribution), then empowered his successor, who would build it. (One of Clinton's strongest finishing-well indicators is how leaders handle succession.)

---

[31] Eugene H. Peterson. (1980). *A Long Obedience in the Same Direction: Discipleship in an Instant Society.* Downers Grove, IL: InterVarsity Press.

David teaches us that finishing well is not finishing flawlessly. Most of us have made costly mistakes along our journey. But that doesn't mean we can't make lasting contributions. The question is whether we are using this season to leave a legacy. God testifies regarding David in Acts 13:36 (NIV), "For David, after he had served God's purpose in his own generation, fell asleep, and was buried." I want this testimony.

6. Sense of destiny fulfilled: Leaders who finish well walk with a growing awareness of a sense of destiny and see some or all of it fulfilled by the end of their lives. Throughout their journey, they carry a sense of divine purpose for their life that often grows stronger over time. This calling gives them direction, resilience, and endurance.

Finishers tend to be purpose-driven leaders: they know what mission they are called to, and they persevere in it. When they reach the latter stages of life, there is a deep satisfaction that they have run the race set before them. This doesn't imply they had an easy journey or achieved everything they dreamed, but they have the assurance that they didn't waste the calling of God on their life.

The Danger Zones

The primary pitfalls that threaten our finishing well can be summed up in 1 John 2:16: "the desires of the flesh and the desires of the eyes and pride of life." Essentially, issues of sex, money, and pride trip up leaders along the way—misuse of finances, abuse of power, pride and selfishness, sexual misconduct, family failures, and plateauing are what Clinton found to be the most common poisons to finishing well.

Clinton also identified recurring late-life derailers:

1. Unresolved inner-life issues. Early success masks wounds, pride, insecurity, or drivenness that surface later.
2. Loss of teachability. Leaders stop learning, stop listening, or stop submitting to God's shaping.
3. Power retention. Leaders cling to roles, platforms, or control instead of releasing authority.
4. Lack of relational investment. Ministry outpaces intimacy—marriages, friendships, and mentoring atrophy.
5. Failure to reframe purpose in later seasons. Many leaders never discern a winter assignment—they try to live forever in summer.

Barnabas's Finale

In the final years of his winter season, Barnabas probably made Salamis, Cyprus, his primary ministry location. He strengthened churches, discipled believers and leaders, and evangelized Jewish audiences. He may have written, but if so his writings have been lost in history. He did not seek prominence but leveraged his spiritual wisdom and experience to multiply and build the Church.

Tradition tells us Barnabas was stoned to death by hostile Jews. He died as a martyr for the Gospel message he had lived and preached. Less probable but repeated often in church tradition is the idea that John Mark buried Barnabas outside Salamis with a copy of Matthew's Gospel in his hands.

Barnabas exemplifies a multiplier who had significant direct impact but even greater indirect impact through the leaders he empowered. In a list of New Testament heroes, Barnabas is often forgotten. My guess is that Barnabas wouldn't even care. He would rather see one of his spiritual son's or daughter's names on the list than his own. This is the heart of a multiplier.

Aunt Helga and the Spirit of Caleb

At 100 years of age, Deb's godly Great-Aunt Helga had her
driver's license taken away. Her kids refused to let her drive any
longer. Aunt Helga complained, "You can't take my driver's
license away because who is going to pick up all those old
people on Sundays and take them to church?" Helga had been
doing this ministry for 40 years. At age 110, Aunt Helga finished
well.

As Ashley Montagu writes, "The idea is to die young … as late
as possible."[32]

My prayer for my last season of life is that I would have the
spirit of Caleb. Caleb was 85 years old when he finally entered
the promised land—still strong, still believing, still confronting
giants, and still taking territory for the Kingdom of God. He
demonstrates that faithfulness over time positions leaders to
finish strong rather than fade away. Leaders must begin with the
end in mind and learn to "number our days, that we may gain a
heart of wisdom" (Psalm 90:12).

Multiplier Insight: Finishing

Leaders who multiply start and journey with the goal of
finishing well. I often have leaders write their own eulogy. What
do you want the significant others in your life to say at your
funeral? What are you doing today to live in a way they can

---

[32] Ashley Montagu, quoted in discussions of aging and vitality; see especially
his broader reflections on lifelong growth in *The Meaning of Love* (New York:
Harper & Brothers, 1953). The phrase "The idea is to die young … as late
as possible" is commonly attributed to Montagu as a representative aphorism
rather than a formally published line.

honestly say these things? Don't make the preacher lie at your
funeral.

Whatever season you are in, cultivate the values, habits, relationships, and ministry philosophy that will make you a multiplier. Remember that leadership is a marathon, pace yourself, and make choices that will help you still be running strong at
the finish.

CONCLUSION
The Multiplier's Legacy

Our book began with the honest observation that the Church has a mission math problem. For those who are engaged in the Kingdom mission of disciple-making, the vast majority are doing addition. We have made the argument that the solution to our problem is found in mission multiplication. We believe with all our hearts that God's plan for us is to develop over the seasons of our lives for multiplication ministry.

You can keep struggling in disappointment, trying to add more people to your church to break the 200 barrier so you can be in the elite 8% of churches in America. Or you can do what Jesus, Peter, Barnabas, and Paul did: give your attention to making disciples and leaders out of ordinary folks who actually multiply. Then the Kingdom will grow, even if your church doesn't (but usually it will).

Your life and leadership are unfolding in a "unique season story." Scripture teaches this. Creation declares it. Wisdom confirms it. Research verifies it. Yet leadership literature—and often Christian ministry—have been strangely resistant to this truth. Experts speak often about calling, vision, strategy, and fruitfulness. They speak far less about timing, investment, transition, or the faith required to grow during our seasons and then to release one season so another can begin. They speak even more rarely about pursuing multiplication through those seasons.

John and I have sought to explain that multiplication—of disciples, leaders, churches, and Kingdom impact—does not happen accidentally. Multiplication demands intentionality, tenacity, and a refusal to settle for the short-term win that quickly fades. It requires a faith in the long-term Kingdom fruitfulness that maximizes your legacy.

In this way, Barnabas stands not as an unattainable hero like Paul, but as an accessible model—especially for leaders who may never be "the one in a thousand" but who quietly shape dozens who go on to shape thousands.

Barnabas was not the most gifted leader in the early church. He certainly wasn't the most prominent. He wrote no New Testament letters. He preached no sermons we can quote. He led no movement that bears his name. Yet, few figures in Scripture better embody the life of a true multiplier—one who prioritized encouraging and empowering other leaders, whose influence far outlived his visibility, and whose greatest contribution was not what he built but "who he sent."

Barnabas's life, when viewed through the lens of seasons and leadership development, becomes more than a biography. It becomes a pattern. A map. A mirror.

And when his story is read alongside the insights of Robert Clinton, one truth becomes unavoidable: the leaders who finish well are those who learn to steward each season faithfully—then let it go and move forward, multiplying at every stage.

Seasons Are Not Stages to Conquer, But Gifts to Steward

One of the quiet assumptions this book has challenged is the idea that leadership is a straight line of progress—more responsibility, more authority, more visibility, more impact. Clinton's research dismantles this myth. Leadership development, he insists, is nonlinear. It includes growth, yes—but also pruning, redirection, and often painful redefinition. Has anyone reading this gone through some pain, some redefinition, some refinement, some redirection in ministry? John has. I have. Barnabas did. Moses did.

Moses, for all his failures, is a keen example of this. Forty years in the palace. Forty years in the sheep fields. Forty years in the wilderness. Empowering and handing off leadership to his apprentice, Joshua, who will finish the mission. Hiking up Mount Nebo to die but seeing the promised land. Reappearing with the new "Joshua," Jesus, on another mountain, the Mount of Transfiguration. Being honored as a hero of the faith who finished well, despite his stumbling. He stewarded his seasons through the peaks and valleys. So can you.

The four seasons framework—spring, summer, autumn, winter—offers language for this reality.

Spring is the season of planting, preparation, and calling. Vision is forming faster than fruit.
Summer is the season of growth and ministry experimentation. Capacity expands, ministries form, and fruit increases.
Autumn is the season of harvesting, using all God has built in you and taught you to make your significant contribution. The leader's role gradually shifts from doing to a priority on developing.
Winter is the season of legacy, transfer, and trust. Influence deepens even as visibility decreases.

Each season carries both opportunity and temptation. The temptation is always the same: to cling to what once worked, to confuse fruitfulness with faithfulness, or to refuse the grief that usually accompanies sending and transition.

Finishing Well Starts Now

Robert Clinton's research confirms what Barnabas's life illustrates: finishing well is not a single decision made late in life. It is the cumulative effect of decisions made faithfully across decades.

Clinton speaks of "convergence"—when calling, gifts, experience, and opportunity align. But he also speaks of afterglow—the season when a leader's greatest contribution is not expansion, but transfer.

This is where many leaders falter. We are often trained for spring and summer. We study for growth. We strategize for expansion. That's the addition ethos. But we are rarely discipled for empowering others and releasing. That's the multiplication ethos. We do not talk enough about how to step aside without stepping away, how to bless successors without overshadowing them, how to measure fruit when our names are no longer attached to it.

Barnabas models this beautifully. He never confuses relevance or popularity with faithfulness. He understands that the goal of leadership is not longevity or "likes" but Kingdom multiplication—the kind that continues when you are gone, your maximum Kingdom legacy.

Multiplication Is the Only Strategy That Survives the Seasons

Strategies shift. Programs end. Buildings age. Ministries have life cycles. Movements stall. But multiplication—when done relationally and intentionally—outlives every season.

Multiplication is not simply growth by addition. It is growth by reproduction. It requires time, patience, trust, and often hidden work. It demands leaders who are secure enough to give away what they have earned.

This is why multiplication cannot be rushed, and it cannot be faked.

It begins in spring, when leaders learn before they lead.

It accelerates in summer, when leadership is shared and teams are formed.

It matures in autumn, when authority is transferred and others are celebrated.

It endures in winter, when you plant in others all God has given you, and Kingdom legacy outlives you.

Barnabas lived this pattern. He was a healthy disciple-making leader who championed reproduction.

In a world obsessed with immediacy and visibility, the multiplier chooses faithfulness over fame.

In a culture that rewards control, the multiplier practices release.

In an era anxious about decline, the multiplier plants seeds they may never see mature.

The Invitation: Discern Your Season, Decide Your Legacy

The most important question is not, "What season am I in?" It is, "Am I responding to this season faithfully?" How am I championing reproduction in this season?

At every stage, the temptation is to live in yesterday's anointing rather than today's assignment. Multipliers resist that temptation. They allow God to redefine fruitfulness again and again.

A Final Word to Leaders

The solution to the Church's math problem is multiplication. The solution is you and me! The time is now!

Consider this: as of this writing, if I live to the median age of an American male, I have about 15 years left. If John does the same, he has about 30 years left. That's enough time for me to start a multiplication chain of disciples that's 1,000+ when I die. But John could potentially have over 250,000 in his legacy chain. That's using the math in our introduction—three years for three disciples who repeat the pattern with others. The point is, whatever season you are in, start now! It's not too early, and it's not too late.

The true impact of your life will not be the size of what you built but the strength of what continues without you. Disciples, leaders, ministries, and churches thrive and multiply because you invest deeply, empower fully, and release trustingly.

May you discern your season. May you learn and lead during it faithfully. When the time comes, may you release what you love—trusting that God's work is always larger than any one life. May you finish well and maximize your Kingdom legacy!

That is the way of Barnabas. That is the wisdom of the seasons. And that is the power of a true multiplier.

Multipliers maximize their Kingdom legacy by growing through their seasons and sowing seeds into the lives of others.

MULTIPLIER COVENANT

By God's grace, and to advance God's Kingdom, I commit to pursuing the life of a Multiplier — a healthy, disciple-making leader who champions reproduction-knowing that you reproduce who you are and what you do.

HEALTHY
(INTERIOR WORLD)

I commit to prioritizing my relational, physical, mental/emotional, and spiritual well-being as the foundation of fruitful leadership. By living a Christ-centered life, I aim to lead authentically and resiliently, by routinely checking these four internal gauges:

— My RELATIONAL *gauge: Am I investing in healthy, life-giving relationships?*
— My PHYSICAL *gauge: Am I caring for my body with rest, movement, and margin?*
— My MENTAL *gauge: Am I cultivating focus, clarity, and resilience?*
— My SPIRITUAL *gauge: Am I staying rooted in the presence and power of God?*

DISCIPLE-MAKING LEADER
WHO CHAMPIONS REPRODUCTION
(EXTERIOR WORLD)

I am committed to living as a disciple of Jesus and advancing the mission to multiply disciples around the world. I will lead with humility and serve others, striving to be Spirit-led in all that I do. I will prioritize reproduction, collaboration, and unity in Kingdom work, trusting in God's plans and empowering others to step into their unique callings. I am committed to consistently pursue the 4 practices of a Multiplier:

— MAKE DISCIPLE MAKERS: *I will personally disciple others in ways that multiply.*
— ESTABLISH SPIRITUAL COMMUNITIES: *I will help start and strengthen communities that center around Jesus.*
— MOBILIZE NEW LEADERS: *I will identify and empower emerging leaders.*
— LAUNCH CHURCH EXPRESSIONS: *I will send leaders and support the launch of new church expressions wherever God leads.*

My commitment to multiplication is fueled by a vision for Jesus' mission and to see the church restored to its movemental form *all over the world.*

This covenant is made before God and my friends on mission, seeking His grace to fulfill this sacred call. I trust in His strength, wisdom, and guidance as I walk forward in faith and surrender.

COMMIT HERE ⟶